Accountability Among
Senior Civil Servants

Accountability Among Senior Civil Servants

Mary Daly

INSTITUTE OF PUBLIC ADMINISTRATION

First published 1987
by the Institute of Public Administration
57–61 Lansdowne Road, Dublin 4

ISBN 0 906980 80 1

Mary Daly has published **A Report on the Alcohol Education Court
Programme** (Stationery Office, 1983), **The West Limerick Study** (with J.
O'Connor, Social Research Centre, 1983), **The World of the Elderly: The
Rural Experience** (with J. O'Connor, National Council for the Aged,
1984), **The Smoking Habit** (with J. O'Connor, Gill and Macmillan,
1985), **The Hidden Workers** (Employment Equality Agency, 1985),
**Towards Forward Planning – An Evaluation of the Pilot COMTEC
Programme** (with Laraine Joyce, Institute of Public Administration,
1987).

Printed in Ireland by Criterion Press Limited, Dublin

CONTENTS

TABLES

FIGURES

ACRONYMS

The following are the main acronyms used in this text:

C & AG : Office of the Comptroller and Auditor General

DPS : Department of the Public Service

HEO : Higher Executive Officer

MAC : Management Advisory Committee

PAC : Committee of Public Accounts

PQs : Parliamentary Questions

ACKNOWLEDGMENTS

_____

This study was commissioned and financed by the former Department of the Public Service on the advice of the Committee for Administrative Research. The support and advice of the Department and the Committee are gratefully acknowledged. The contribution of the former chairperson of the Committee, Des Kelly, deserves special mention.

The key contributors to the study were the eighty-four senior civil servants who comprised the respondent population. The study would not have been possible without their generous cooperation and help.

The helpful comments given by Dr. Richard Sinnott of University College, Dublin are gratefully acknowledged.

Within the Institute of Public Administration, special thanks are due to Pat Hall, Deputy Director General, for his continued support and constructive comments on earlier drafts. I am particularly indebted to my colleague, Laraine Joyce, whose knowledge of civil service management structures and practices contributed in a major way to the study. Special thanks are also due to Evelyn Blennerhassett. Richard Boyle made helpful

comments at the drafting stage. The excellent
secretarial and administrative assistance provided by
Deborah Adams, Caroline Byrne and Breeda Doyle deserves
special mention. Their skill, cheerfulness and patience
greatly aided the preparation of this work. Jonathan
Williams gave expert help in editing the report.

All errors of fact and opinion contained in the following
pages remain my responsibility.

Mary Daly

1 November, 1987

Chapter One

A STUDY OF CHANGING ACCOUNTABILITY

_____

1.1 Focus of Study

This study focuses on the accountability of senior
civil servants in Ireland. It describes the measures
used to effect accountability in the Irish civil
service and senior civil servants' perceptions of and
reactions to these measures. Particular attention is
paid to the perceived impact of accountability
mechanisms introduced since 1983, the kinds of
problems experienced and the policy issues raised by
the new emphasis on increased accountability in the
Irish civil service generally.

1.2 Study Background and Objectives

Civil servants now operate in an environment that is
markedly different from that of the past. Two of the
most important factors contributing to this change
are the financial constraints under which modern
government operates and the changing expectations
that the public and politicians have of the civil

service. Value for money has become a primary
concern. In addition, the machinery of public
administration has become much more complex, leading
to an increased recognition of the importance and
necessity of putting in place adequate accountability
mechanisms.

In Ireland, the pressure towards increased
accountability is evidenced by a number of recent
developments, three of which are:
- the increased use of Select Oireachtas
  Committees, especially the setting up of the
  Committee on Public Expenditure in 1983
- the establishment of the Office of the Ombudsman
  in 1984
- the former government's White Paper of September
  1985, Serving the Country Better, which
  advocates a new system of departmental
  management, in which accountability is a key
  element.

It was against this changing background that the
present study was commissioned by the former
Department of the Public Service in 1985.

The objectives of the study are:

- to identify the formal structures and procedures of accountability amongst the highest ranks of the civil service and the changes that have occurred in recent years
- to elicit the perceptions of senior civil servants of how accountability operates and to examine their reactions to: the prescriptions in the White Paper, Serving the Country Better, that relate to managerial accountability, the Committee on Public Expenditure, and the Office of the Ombudsman
- to examine the reported influence of each of these developments and to identify potential areas of difficulty in implementing measures designed to increase the accountability of senior civil servants.

1.3 Definition of Accountability

Accountability is a word that can have a number of different meanings. To clarify the concept, it is helpful to link it to the notion of stewardship, which is established when one party entrusts another with resources and/or responsibilities.(1) Accountability implies two things: the existence of some authority or person to whom account has to be given; and the performance of actions that have to be accounted for. Accountability and responsibility are closely related and may be regarded as two dimensions of the same relationship.(2)

Although accountability and financial accounting are frequently equated, financial accounting is just one dimension of the accountability framework within which a civil servant operates. Senior civil servants can be held accountable in a variety of ways. The three developments that are the focus of this study suggest that there are at least two constituencies to which they may be accountable:

- accountability to the internal administrative system, to which the 1985 White Paper was addressed

- accountability to the parliamentary system, effected directly through ministers and the Oireachtas Committees and indirectly through the Office of the Ombudsman.

The study examines how these mechanisms of accountability operate and explores the kinds of procedures and interactions to which they give rise among the higher echelons of the civil service.

1.4 Method of Study

A review of the literature on the topic of accountability and contacts initiated with research agencies abroad revealed that, at that time, no empirical research on the impact of accountability mechanisms on the work of senior civil servants had been undertaken in the United Kingdom and most European countries. It is therefore not possible to compare or contrast the findings of this study with those of other studies.

The primary method of data collection was semi-structured interviewing. A briefing document was circulated to each government department or office and an interview schedule was developed and tested during pilot work. The fieldwork for the study was carried out over a six-month period between August 1985 and January 1986. The study does not, therefore, take into account any of the changes that were introduced after January 1986.

Respondents were drawn from the ranks of the senior civil service --- senior civil servants being defined as office-holders at the principal officer grade and above. Not all senior civil servants have had contact with the Committee on Public Expenditure or the Office of the Ombudsman. Consequently, respondents were selected from those who had some personal experience of these two relatively recent accountability mechanisms. Respondents ranged across departments and grades, but at least one staff member from twenty-five departments, offices and commissions was interviewed. Wherever possible, chief professional and technical officers were also interviewed.

In all, eighty-four senior civil servants were interviewed. Their grade breakdown was as follows:

Secretary	16
Head of Office/Commission	6
Second/Deputy Secretary	4
Assistant Secretary	28
Principal Officer	30

The study was favourably received and 95 per cent of those who were approached agreed to be interviewed.

Given the qualitative nature of the data, statistical analysis was inappropriate, and all data were coded and analysed manually. For the purpose of analysis and to preserve confidentiality, respondents were classified into three grade categories: (i) heads of departments (which included departmental secretaries and heads of offices or commissions), (ii) deputy/ assistant secretaries and (iii) principal officers. Professional and technical respondents were categorised into their equivalent general service grade.

1.5 Content of Report

Chapter Two describes the formal structures and procedures used to effect accountability in the Irish civil service and outlines the changes that have been made in recent years. Chapter Three describes how senior civil servants perceive accountability to operate in practice. Chapter Four looks at accountability within departments, focusing specifically on the perceived impact of the 1985 White Paper's framework for accountable management. The focus in Chapter Five is on the operation and impact of the Committee on Public Expenditure. Chapter Six examines the operation of the Office of the Ombudsman and outlines senior civil servants' experience and perceptions of that Office. The final chapter reviews the study's main findings and discusses a number of key issues. A bibliography accompanies the text.

REFERENCES

1. A. Gray develops the idea of stewardship in 'Codes of accountability and the presentation of an account: Towards a micro-administrative theory of public accountability,' Public Administration Bulletin 46 (December 1984): 2-13.

2. S. Maheshwari, 'Accountability in public administration: Towards a conceptual framework,' Indian Journal of Public Administration, Vol. XXIX (3 : 1983): 457-472.

Chapter Two

THE FORMAL FRAMEWORK FOR ACCOUNTABILITY
AND SOME RECENT REFORMS

2.1 Introduction

This chapter describes the formal structures and
procedures used to effect accountability in the Irish
civil service and outlines the changes that have been
made in recent years. It is based on available
literature and legal documentation. The chapter is
divided into two sections. The first outlines
traditional or classical structures and procedures
for accountability, while the second section
discusses the pursuit of reform and summarises the
major initiatives that took place between 1966 and
1985.

Since Ireland is a parliamentary democracy with a
written constitution that provides for the
traditional separation of powers between the
legislature, executive and judiciary, accountability
is a central element in the country's administrative

system. Its application has been shaped largely by the British tradition, which involves principles and procedures dating from the seventeenth century.

In discussing accountability mechanisms in Ireland's public administration, it is useful to distinguish between three forms of control: <u>parliamentary control,</u> which is effected through Dáil Éireann; <u>judicial or legal control,</u> which is effected through the courts; and <u>administrative control,</u> which is exercised internally in government departments and offices.

Parliamentary and judicial control may be viewed as external accountability mechanisms, in contrast to administrative control, which is internal in nature. The different procedures that are used to effect these types of accountability are outlined in the following sections.

2.2 How Parliamentary Control is Exercised

Parliamentary control is exercised in two main ways:

1. ministerial accountability to the parliament

2. parliamentary enquiry and surveillance.

The first is directed to the political executive

(i.e., the government), while the second is largely
the responsibility of the civil service.

2.2.1 Executive and Ministerial Accountability to Parliament

Ministers are held accountable to the Dáil by means
of parliamentary questions, debates on the estimates
for their departments, motions moved by members of
the Dáil, and whenever they are proposing legislation
to give additional powers or funds to any public
body.(1) Ministerial accountability is not only one
of the central principles of the traditional
framework of accountability but is acknowledged to be
a main determinant of how the civil service
operates.(2)

Legally, it is the government administration, not the
civil service per se, that is subject to
parliamentary control. In law, the civil service is
seen to play a subservient role in the service of the
government.(3) Parliamentary control in the civil
service is, therefore, indirect in nature, occurring
through ministers and the government.

The most important legislation governing the
accountability of civil servants is the Ministers and

Secretaries Act 1924-1980. Under this Act, the minister is the 'corporation sole' or legal personality of the department. Legal powers, with very few exceptions, are conferred on him/her and, to be validly exercised, must be performed under his/her direction. This individual responsibility of ministers to the Dáil for the operation of their departments means that they may be required to account for the activities of civil servants working under them. The relationship between a minister and his/her civil servants is founded therefore upon the legal stipulation that the minister is the source of authority in the department.

This centralised system of ministerial power is in contrast to systems that prevail in France and some other European countries. In France, for example, the bureaucracy is more directly accountable to the people through administrative courts and quasi-judicial offices.

2.2.2 Parliamentary Enquiry and Surveillance

Parliamentary enquiry is mainly ex post facto in nature. The process of auditing and the operation of various parliamentary committees of enquiry are the principal means used to effect this kind of accountability. There exists a very elaborate system of parliamentary control in relation to finance, so much so that it could be said that finance has provided the focus of parliamentary accountability.

The most important exception to the doctrine of ministerial responsibility occurs in the fiscal area, viz. the special position of the accounting officer. The accounting officer is the person appointed by the Minister for Finance (under Section 22 of the <u>Exchequer and Audit Departments Act 1866)</u> to be responsible to the Dáil (through the Committee of Public Accounts) for the proper expenditure of money voted to his or her department.(4) The accounting officer is personally responsible for the safeguarding of public funds and property under his or her control, for the regularity and propriety of all the transactions in each appropriation account bearing his or her signature, and also for the efficiency and economy of administration in his or her department. The accounting officer is usually the head of the department, office or commission and is accountable in financial matters to the Dail rather than to the minister.

The independence of the accounting officer role from the minister is specified in the 1866 Act. In the case of a difference of opinion between an accounting officer and a minister on the propriety of a payment, the accounting officer must inform the minister in writing of his or her view and of the reason for it and suggest a consultation with the Department of Finance. If the minister gives written instructions to proceed, the Accounting Officer should comply with them after informing the Department of Finance, and should communicate the relevant documentation to the Comptroller and Auditor General when the minister's instructions have been carried out. When called upon, the accounting officer must appear before the Committee of Public Accounts to answer for the correctness of each account and explain any matters arising. He or she may be held personally liable to make good any sum that the Committee disallows.

Audit is central to parliamentary control since the objective of financial accountability is to check that the intentions of the legislature are not flouted through illegalities, irregularities, improprieties or wastefulness. The legal basis for the auditing process is set down in the Exchequer and

Audit Departments Acts of 1866 and 1921 and
in Article 22 of the Constitution. (5)

There are two key agents of parliamentary control
over financial affairs: the Comptroller and Auditor
General and the Committee of Public Accounts, each
engaging in an independent scrutiny of public
expenditure.

The Comptroller and Auditor General Act 1923
established the framework of statutory control of the
auditing process. Holding office under Article 33 of
the 1937 Constitution, the Comptroller and Auditor
General is a servant of the Dáil, not the government,
and he must report to the Dáil. His role is
twofold: (i) to control all issues of money from the
Exchequer on behalf of the state; and (ii) to audit
the government accounts for accuracy and regularity
and to report on them to the Dáil, drawing attention
to any misappropriation, waste or uneconomic
expenditure.

The Committee of Public Accounts is the second key
agent of parliamentary control over financial
affairs. This select committee of the Dáil is
appointed (under standing order 126 of the House) for

the examination of the appropriation accounts for a particular year. First established in 1922, the Committee is empowered to examine and report to the Dail upon the appropriation accounts and to suggest alterations and improvements in the form of the estimates submitted to the Dáil. The Comptroller and Auditor General is permanently in attendance at the meetings and the Committee bases its review largely on his report. The principal witnesses are the accounting officers; an officer of the Department of Finance is also in attendance. When it concludes its examination of the accounts for a particular year, the Committee presents its final report publicly to the Dáil. Neither the departments concerned nor the Department of Finance are consulted at the drafting stage. A formal reply to the report is prepared by the Department of Finance in consultation with other departments. The government is not obliged to accept the recommendations of the Committee's report.

In addition to the Comptroller and Auditor General and the Committee of Public Accounts, other Oireachtas Committees may question senior civil servants on relevant issues, but they have no legal powers to hold civil servants to account.

2.3 How Judicial Control is Exercised

Judicial control of the government derives from the Constitution, which provides for courts, including those empowered to adjudicate on the constitutionality of a law. This means that the government and the civil service are amenable to the law. A civil servant has no special immunity from prosecution in either the civil or the criminal courts, but the powers of the court are limited. The courts cannot intervene, provided an authority entrusted with administrative discretion keeps within its powers and (where appropriate) commits no open breach of natural justice.(6)

Judicial control is, therefore, less significant than the parliamentary system as a means of effecting operational accountability from the administration. The court's role in relation to the administration is indirect: it may ensure that public bodies carry out their business with full regard to the concept of 'natural justice'. It is also within the power of the judiciary to clarify the meaning of the law where there is a conflict between a citizen and the administration and to review how the law has helped to resolve it.(7)

2.4 How Administrative Control is Exercised

Within the Irish civil service, internal
administrative control is exercised in two main
ways:

- intradepartmentally, through the internal
  hierarchy of each department, office or
  commission
- interdepartmentally, by the control departments
  (Finance and the Taoiseach) over the line
  departments and offices or commissions.

Within departments, all civil servants are
accountable to the minister, their relationship being
founded on the legal requirement that the minister is
ultimately responsible for the exercise of powers and
the performance of duties within his/her department.
In constitutional theory the civil servant's loyalty
to the minister is undivided.(8) How this is
realised within a department is not specified in
legislation. Indeed, the law is a poor guide to the
organisation and operation of responsibilities within
a department (except for the financial function). In
theory it is clear: ministers make policy and take
decisions, civil servants execute them. Yet in

practice the literature literature suggests that the
situation is much more complex.(9)

Interdepartmentally, the Department of Finance, and
to a lesser extent the Department of the Taoiseach,
coordinate and control many of the activities of
other departments.

The Department of Finance plays a key role in
exercising administrative control, particularly
financial control, of the civil service. It is
empowered to administer the public finances and also
(under the Economic Planning and Development Order
1980) to review the structures and procedures adopted
by other civil service departments and offices. It
is responsible for the spending of all departments.
In this regard, it issues guidelines for departmental
spending, reviews all estimates and accounts, and
(through the Minister for Finance) is the sanctioning
authority for all expenditures from the public
finances. To give effect to this control, the
Department of Finance has set up a detailed monthly
expenditure reporting system.*

---

* The Comptroller and Auditor General also exercises
a control function, but he is technically not part
of the civil service, being a servant of the Dail.

The second area of administrative control that is exercised by the Department of Finance over other departments relates to personnel policy and organisational issues.* The Department of Finance is the controlling authority in the civil service in all matters relating to pay, superannuation, general conditions of employment, industrial relations and recruitment policy. It is also responsible for developing and regulating management systems and structures throughout the civil service. In this regard, it regularly seeks information from other departments on personnel and organisational matters.

The role of the Department of the Taoiseach, which acts as the secretariat to the government, is primarily coordinative --- acting mainly as a channel of communication between civil service departments, the government and other state institutions.

Apart from these official intradepartmental and interdepartmental controls, civil service departments are also subject to other less direct and formal sources of influence --- principally from the media,

---

* This task was formerly carried out by the Department of the Public Service, established in 1973 and subsumed into the Department of Finance in 1987.

interest groups, and individual politicians, both national and local.(10) Although they have no specific authority, these influences cannot be ignored or neglected in a democratic system.

2.5 The Accountability Debate

The need for organisational and structural change in the Irish civil service has been recognised for many years and various initiatives have been implemented since the publication of the first major report of the Public Services Organisation Review Group in 1966.(11) In 1986, total government expenditure amounted to £9.8 billion (12) and the number of governmental and quasi-governmental bodies exceeded 400. These figures have given a new impetus to the concept of public accountability and have focused attention on the effectiveness of existing controls. There is a strong belief, both inside and outside the public administrative system, that traditional structures of accountability are in need of radical overhaul.

In the wide-ranging debate about the effectiveness of the administration in changing times, two themes have been dominant:

- the shortcomings of traditional accounting
  procedures and methods
- the efficacy of the doctrine of ministerial
  responsibility.

The traditional accounting system, focusing as it
does on regularity and propriety, is criticised on
three main fronts.

First, the system of accounting on a votes basis does
not allow for information on the total cost of
providing particular services. Therefore, the
information system itself is perceived to be
inadequate.(13) Second, since existing
accountability procedures are oriented to operational
control, they have limited capacity to embrace the
general output or impact of expenditure.(14) A
suggested remedy for this is that accountability
should transcend the custodial function to encompass
responsibility for both effectiveness and
efficiency. Third, the present budgetary system is
criticised since it is based largely on expenditure
patterns established over time. This, it is argued,
leads to inbuilt resistance to change and in the
medium-term militates against national planning of
expenditure.(15)

The second major focus of criticism has been the
doctrine of ministerial responsibility and the
convention of the 'corporation sole'. The main
reservation expressed in relation to this has been
the difficulty of holding a minister responsible for
all the actions of his or her departmental officials,
especially in times of increasingly complex
government. C.H. Murray goes so far as to call it a
'legal fiction'; for Smyth it is an 'archaic
doctrine'.(16)

2.6 Progress in Reform: 1966-86

The setting up of the Public Services Organisation
Review Group in 1966 marked the onset of the first
formal review of the Irish system of public
administration. Progress in implementing its
proposals has been slow. The changes that have taken
place have tended to be relatively minor and
operational, with one exception perhaps: the setting
up of the Department of the Public Service (DPS) in
1973 as the central coordinating department for the
civil service.* The same Act (The Ministers and
Secretaries (Amendment) Act 1973) established the
Public Service Advisory Council, with the statutory

---

* This innovation was relatively shortlived with the
  integration of the DPS into the Department of
  Finance in 1987.

function to advise the Minister of the Public Service
on the organisation of the public service and on
matters relating to personnel policy. Subsequent
changes have tended to be of an incremental nature
but an identifiable programme of civil service reform
could be said to be now underway.

There have been two main elements to the
modernisation programme:
- measures to improve the internal efficiency of
  the civil service, based on improved information
  systems and management practices
- measures to increase the accountability of the
  civil service to some external agencies.

Figure 2.1 lists the initiatives to achieve these
objectives that had been introduced up to the time of
this study. Three main strategies can be discerned:
- reducing staff numbers in the civil service
- improving management practices and procedures,
  including promoting the concept of personal
  responsibility and accountability
- introducing more external scrutiny of the
  administration's actions and decisions.

Figure 2.1   Measures Introduced to Improve Efficiency
and Effectiveness in the Civil Service :
1981-85

LEVEL	MEASURE	GOAL
INTERNAL	Public Service Embargo on Recruitment 1981	To reduce staff numbers by filling only one in three vacancies
	Guidelines for Financial Management 1984	To increase efficiency and effectiveness by introducing a standardised system of budget costing and review of all departmental activities
	Total management system as proposed in the White Paper, Serving the Country Better 1985	To increase efficiency and effectiveness by introducing management systems based on departmental and individual goal-setting, monitoring of performance, and the systematic analysis of each manager's contribution
EXTERNAL	Committee on Public Expenditure 1983	To review the justification for and effectiveness of ongoing public expenditure
	Office of the Ombudsman 1984	To provide the public with a means of independent investigation of decisions or actions taken by government departments and offices, local authorities, health boards and the telecommunications and postal services.

2.7 Measures to Improve the Internal Efficiency of the Civil Service

The three most important initiatives taken in recent years to improve the efficiency of the civil service relate to (a) a public service embargo on recruitment, (b) modernised financial management systems and (c) better management practices, including goal-setting and performance appraisal.

(a) Public Service Embargo on Recruitment (1981)

In 1981, the government directed that in general only a third of vacancies normally arising in the civil service could be filled. Some measure of the impact of this directive can be gauged from the fact that a 6.5 per cent reduction took place in manning levels in the civil service in the first two full years of its implementation (1982 and 1983) (17). A total embargo on recruitment and promotions in the public service was introduced on 31 March 1987.

(b) Guidelines for Financial Management (1984)

The intent of the Guidelines for Financial Management, introduced in 1984, is to supplement the existing vote accounting practices with a modern financial management system that identifies, monitors and standardises the costings of sets of activities.

The Department of Finance's main concern in the
Guidelines is to develop systems of financial
planning and control throughout the public service.
Taking into consideration both the external and
internal accounting needs of departments, the aim of
this system is to provide regular and standardised
information and analyses of the total cost of
providing various services and activities.

The Guidelines identify stages in implementing
the new system and these cover budgeting, costing an
the comparison of actual performance with budgets on
an activity and responsibility basis. The Guideline
also envisaged a stronger emphasis on internal audit
Departments were also urged to adopt procedures to
ensure a rolling review of their expenditure
programmes.

(c) White Paper, Serving the Country Better (1985)
The White Paper, Serving the Country Better, was lai
before the Houses of the Oireachtas in September
1985. It sets out a management framework for the
Irish civil service based on the principles of
increased delegation of authority and responsibility

to individual senior civil servants. The White Paper
puts forward a total management system to complement
the Department of Finance's financial management
systems as follows:

- a clear statement of departmental goals and
  objectives
- prior identification and costing of results
- monitoring of performance in relation to plans
  and budgets
- a systematic assessment of the contribution and
  performance of each manager.

The White Paper presents a set of guidelines rather
than a blueprint. (The former Department of the
Public Service was to provide support and backup to
departments during the implementation of the White
Paper.) The White Paper also outlines the legal and
parliamentary changes that would be necessary to
facilitate the introduction of the new system;
chiefly an amendment to the Ministers and
Secretaries Act 1924 to allow for a derogation from
the minister as the 'corporation sole'. The Dail was
also accorded a role in the scrutiny of departmental
management, through the aegis of a new select
committee --- the Committee of Public Management* ---

---

* This Committee had yet to be set up at the time of
  study.

which was to draw its membership from both the
Committee of Public Accounts and the Committee on
Public Expenditure.

It was envisaged that the implementation of these
policies would broaden the concept of accountability
to incorporate responsibility for all the resources
under a manager's control. The White Paper
represents an attempt to alter the management and
accountability of the civil service from within and
without. It contains different solutions to the
problem of cutting the costs of government. On the
one hand, cash limits and reductions in manpower are
emphasised, while on the other hand, the White Paper
advocates introducing private sector management and
information systems to the civil service.

2.8 Measures to Increase the External Accountability of
    the Civil Service
    As may be seen from Figure 2.1, the two main
    initiatives in relation to external accountability
    that had occurred up to 1985 were (a) the
    establishment of the Committee on Public Expenditure
    in 1983 and (b) the setting up of the Office of the
    Ombudsman in 1984.

(a) <u>Committee on Public Expenditure (1983)</u>

The Committee on Public Expenditure was set up in
June 1983 to review the justification for and
effectiveness of expenditure of government
departments and state agencies outside the remit of
the Joint Committee on Commercial State-sponsored
Bodies. The Committee on Public Expenditure
investigates major policy areas of public expenditure
of government departments and also reviews specific
expenditure items or policies with a view to
eliminating wasteful or obsolete programmes.

Its terms of reference stipulate that the Committee
shall present an annual progress report to the Dail
on its activities and plans. The Committee carries
out its work in a number of ways: by calling as
witnesses relevant departmental staff, generally at
the principal officer grade and above; by engaging
the services of management and other consultants
where appropriate; and by obtaining detailed written
submissions from departments on their management
practices and procedures. Submissions from the
general public are also invited.

During its first three years of operation (1983-86),
the Committee on Public Expenditure carried out

investigations and published reports on such diverse
topics as the servicing of the public debt, control
of capital projects, the fishing industry, costs of
civil service travel and subsistence, and the leasing
of public sector accommodation.

(b) Office of the Ombudsman (1984)

The Ombudsman Act of 1980 provided for an ombudsman
who can investigate, either on his own initiative or
on the basis of a complaint from any member of the
public, actions taken by civil servants and, since
April 1985, of those public servants in health
boards, local authorities and the telecommunications
and postal services. The Ombudsman took up office in
January 1984.

Within his area of jurisdiction, the Ombudsman may
investigate any action that, in his view, was or may
have been: (i) taken without proper authority, (ii)
taken on irrelevant grounds, (iii) the result of
negligence or carelessness, (iv) based on erroneous
or incomplete information, (v) improperly
discriminatory, (vi) based on undesirable
administrative practice, or (vii) otherwise
contrary to fair or sound administration.(18)
Complaints generally have to be made within twelve

months of the alleged action, delay or inaction; and
the complainant must already have taken up the matter
with the relevant department or office and have
exhausted all other redress facilities. The Office
reports to the Houses of the Oireachtas each year
(and if necessary on specific occasions) on
complaints received and the manner in which public
servants have dealt with them.

Investigators are empowered to demand files and to
question relevant parties. In contrast to Britain
and France, where complaints must be submitted
through parliamentary representatives, citizens in
Ireland can invoke the help of the Ombudsman
directly. Thus, the Office of the Ombudsman affects
the accountability of the administration since it can
scrutinise and review departmental actions.

Of the five initiatives outlined above, two --- the
public service embargo on recruitment (1981) and the
introduction of the Guidelines for Financial
Management (1984) --- are outside the scope of the
study since they are not concerned with the
accountability of the civil service. This study
focuses on three recent initiatives that have
significance for the accountability of senior civil

servants: the White Paper, <u>Serving the Country
Better,</u> the Committee on Public Expenditure and the
Office of the Ombudsman. Each of these is discussed
more fully in the following chapters.

REFERENCES

1. T. Barrington, The Irish Administrative System.
   Dublin: Institute of Public Administration, 1980:
   19.

2. ibid., 174.

3. D. Kiely, 'Ministers and departments -- the legal
   dimension: A view' Seirbhís Phoiblí 7 (1:1986)
   : 7-15.

4. An Outline of Irish Financial Procedures. Dublin:
   Stationery Office, n. d.

5. E. O'Halpin, 'The Dáil Committee of Public Accounts
   1961-1980,' Administration 32 (4:1984): 483-511.

6. J. Kelly 'Administrative discretion', Irish Jurist
   1, N.S. (1966): 210 referred to in B. Chubb, The
   Government and Politics of Ireland. London: Longman,
   1982: 322.

7. T. Barrington, The Irish Administrative System,
   op.cit., 174.

8. M. Wright, 'The responsibility of the civil servant
   in Great Britain,' Administration 23 (4:1975) :
   362-395.

9. ibid., 364. T. Mc Namara, 'Ethics and the civil
   service : Is it an issue?,' Seirbhís Phoiblí 7
   (4:1986): 8-14.

10. W. Smyth, 'The responsibility of the civil servant
    in Ireland,' Administration 23 (4:1975) : 346-348.

11. Report of the Public Services Organisation Review
    Group 1966-1969. Dublin: Stationery Office, 1969.

12. Budget '87. Dublin: Stationery Office, 1987.

13. Public Service Advisory Council, Report for the Year
    Ended 31 October 1980. Dublin: Stationery Office,
    1981.

14. P. Clarke, 'Performance evaluation of public sector
    programmes,' Administration 32 (3:1984) : 294-311.

15. Public Service Advisory Council, Report for the Year
    Ended 31 October 1980, op. cit., 4.

16. C.H. Murray, 'A working and changeable instrument,'
    Administration 30 (4:1982) : 52; W. Smyth, 'The
    responsibility of the civil servant in Ireland,' op.
    cit., 343.

17. Public Service Advisory Council, Report for the Year
    Ended October 31 1983. Dublin: Stationery Office,
    1984 : 32.

18. B. Chubb, The Government and Politics of Ireland,
    op. cit., 324

Chapter Three

SENIOR CIVIL SERVANTS' PERCEPTIONS OF HOW ACCOUNTABILITY OPERATES IN PRACTICE

3.1 Introduction

This chapter describes how senior civil servants
perceive accountability to operate in practice:
it summarises their views of what they are
accountable for and to whom, and their perceptions of
the impact of various accountability procedures on
their day-to-day work. Their opinions of how
accountability has changed in recent years and the
perceived effectiveness of existing procedures are
also presented.

3.2 For What Are Senior Civil Servants Accountable?

When senior civil servants were asked to list the
things for which they felt themselves to be
accountable, their replies varied by grade and task.
Departmental secretaries and heads of offices or
commissions defined their accountability primarily in
financial terms, arising from their role as

accounting officer, whereas deputy and assistant secretaries and principal officers defined accountability in relation to their routine/daily responsibilites.

Most secretaries of departments and heads of offices or commissions noted that, legally, it was the minister who was accountable for all departmental matters, other than those of a financial nature. Only 4 of the 16 secretaries who were interviewed stated specifically that they were accountable for the general operation, performance and management of their departments. In contrast, most deputy secretaries, assistant secretaries and principal officers equated accountability with responsibility, perceiving themselves as being technically accountable for those aspects of their work for which they were responsible.

A further difference existed between grades. Secretaries and heads of offices/commissions defined their accountability in relation to the entire department (or office/commission), whereas deputy secretaries, assistant secretaries and principal officers defined their accountability mainly in terms

of their individual operations or those of the
section for which they were responsible.

Field of operation or task also influenced
respondents' perceptions of accountability.
Accountability was thought to be most clearly
delineated by those officers who exercised some kind
of financial responsibility; the procedures in this
case are relatively standardised and long-standing.
Senior civil servants involved in service delivery
found it quite difficult to define their
accountability. Accountability was most complex for
those officers who formulate policy since (a) legally
it is the minister who is accountable for policy-
making and (b) it is difficult to hold an officer
accountable for such an unspecifiable activity as
policy-making.

3.3 To Whom do Senior Civil Servants See Themselves as being Accountable?

Theoretically, three types of accountability exist
for the civil service: parliamentary, judicial and
administrative. However, this study suggests that
the practice deviates some way from the formal
framework. Only parliamentary and administrative
accountability influenced the day-to-day operations

of the senior civil servants who were interviewed.
They perceived accountability to the judicial system
as being quite remote: less than 2 per cent of those
interviewed made any reference to it.

Secretaries and heads of offices or commissions saw
accountability to the parliamentary system, effected
through the minister, as primary, whereas the most
important aspect for deputy and assistant secretaries
and principal officers was their accountability to
the administrative system (Table 3.1). In all, only
6 of the 16 departmental secretaries interviewed
referred to the Committee of Public Accounts when
they were asked a general question about the bodies
or people to whom they saw themselves as being
accountable.

While a fifth of deputy and assistant secretaries
said that they were accountable to the minister, this
grade was normally held to account through the
administrative hierarchy in their particular
department. Principal officers were also held to
account in this way. However, about a fifth of the
principal officers who were interviewed said that
they were directly accountable to the departmental

secretary, while 7 per cent said that they reported directly to the minister.

Table 3.1 Senior Civil Servants' Perceptions of their Primary Source of Accountability, by Grade*

Source	Heads of Departments	Deputy Assistant Secretaries	Principal Officers	Total
Minister	19 (86%)	7 (22%)	2 (7%)	28 (34%)
Dáil	1 (5%)	1 (3%)	–	2 (2%)
Committee of Public Accounts	2 (9%)	–	–	2 (2%)
Sec./Chairman	–	24 (75%)	6 (20%)	30 (36%)
Assistant Sec.	–	–	20 (66%)	20 (24%)
No answer	–	–	2 (7%)	2 (2%)
N	22	32	30	84

* In this and all subsequent tables, the 'Heads of Departments' category includes the sixteen departmental secretaries' and the six heads of the offices or commissions who were interviewed. The 'Deputy/Assistant Secretaries' category is made up of two second secretaries, two deputy secretaries and twenty-eight assistant secretaries.

3.4 How Is Senior Civil Servants' Accountability Effected?

An essential element of accountability in any system is reporting or checking procedures. These vary considerably in practice within the senior civil service. As Table 3.2 indicates, about a quarter of all the senior civil servants who were interviewed

could identify no set or regular procedures whereby
they are held to account.

Table 3.2   Senior Civil Servants' Reports of Whether Set
             Procedures Exist to Effect Accountability,
             by Grade

Set Procedures	Heads of Departments	Deputy/ Assistant Secretaries	Principal Officers	Total
Yes	18 (82%)	27 (84%)	17 (57%)	62 (74%)
No	4 (18%)	5 (16%)	12 (40%)	21 (25%)
No answer	–	–	1 (3%)	1 (1%)
N	22	32	30	84

The top three grades in the civil service experienced
a more formalised system of accountability than the
principal officer grade.   Thus, 18 per cent of heads
of departments said that no specific accountability
procedures existed for them, while this was the case
for 40 per cent of principal officers.

A second interesting finding was the wide variation
that exists in the accountability procedures at work
in the Irish civil service.   Those mentioned include
meetings, written reports, informal contacts, review
of budgets and estimates, and the monitoring of work
schedules.

Administrative and parliamentary accountability must be differentiated further when one looks at how they operate in practice. Each has an internal dimension (i.e., within the department) and an external dimension. In addition, a number of channels exist to effect both administrative and parliamentary accountability.

3.4.1 Internal Administrative Accountability

Internal administrative accountability was effected largely by internal reporting procedures to the management hierarchy within the department. Thus, principal officers generally reported to the assistant secretary who, in turn, reported to the secretary or head of the department or office.

Senior civil servants were held to account within the department in five main ways. They are, in descending order of identified frequency:
- meetings with senior manager(s)
- informal contacts with senior manager(s)
- meetings of the Management Advisory Committee (MAC)
- regular reviews of budgetary estimates
- monitoring of an agreed work schedule.

The use and frequency of each of these procedures varied considerably; little standardisation existed and none was common to all departments at the time of study. The main factor affecting their extent and prevalence was the operating style of the individual secretary, head or other senior manager(s).

(i) <u>Meetings and Informal Contacts:</u> Prearranged meetings with the immediate superior were the most widespread means of effecting accountability within departments. Such meetings were more important for the assistant secretary grade than for any other. Where they occurred, such meetings tended to relate to the processing of current work. Informal contacts with the senior manager(s) were also quite important, especially for holding principal officers to account. Again, these tended to focus on work in progress.

(ii) <u>The MAC:</u> Typically composed of the secretary or head and the assistant secretaries, the MAC's task is to review and monitor the major management and operational issues arising within the department.

Data available suggested that MACs were in operation in eleven departments of state and two offices or commissions at the time this study was carried out. Some of the largest departments engaged in service delivery were among the six departments that did not have a MAC structure. No consistent differences existed between departments with a MAC and those without one. Even where they existed, some MACs were not active; in all, the evidence suggested that only seven departmental MACs regularly reviewed the department's operation and its progress in meeting objectives.

(iii) <u>Reviews of Budgets and Monitoring of Work</u>: Two further procedures for internal administrative accountability were mentioned by respondents: regular internal reviews of budgetary estimates and the monitoring of the individual or section work schedule(s). The former was more important for the assistant secretary grade than for any other. Monitoring of work schedules was the principal form of accountability within the department for about 14 per cent of the study population, comprising roughly even proportions of assistant secretaries and principal officers.

3.4.2 <u>External Administrative Accountability</u>

External administrative accountability is exercised

by control departments or offices within the civil
service, of which there were three at the time of the
study: Department of Finance, Office of the
Comptroller and Auditor General (C & AG) and the (now
former) Department of the Public Service.

Each of these three agents of external administrative
accountability required specific, and for the most
part discrete, reporting activities from
departments. Figure 3.1 sets these out.

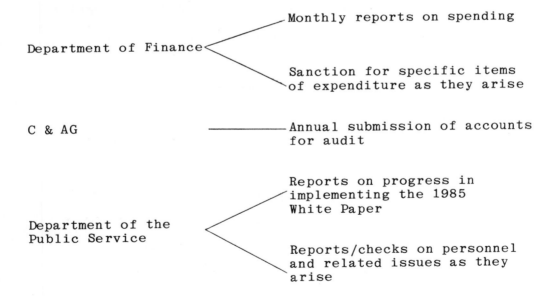

Figure 3.1 Main Procedures for Effecting
External Administrative Accountability

Department of Finance

Monthly reports on spending

Sanction for specific items
of expenditure as they arise

C & AG ——————— Annual submission of accounts
for audit

Department of the
Public Service

Reports on progress in
implementing the 1985
White Paper

Reports/checks on personnel
and related issues as they
arise

(i) <u>Department of Finance:</u> Practices were clearest in the financial area. Since the Department of Finance issued the <u>Guidelines for Financial Management</u> in 1984, departments had been working towards a system for costing their programmes so as to assess the value derived from expenditure.

As part of this financial management system, departments compiled and submitted the details of their expenditure each month to the Department of Finance. Departments also sought the sanction of the Department of Finance for expenditures in excess of certain amounts. The frequency of this form of contact varied across departments, being most widespread in the larger departments. In general, the Department of Finance was felt to exert very strong budgetary control over line departments.

(ii) <u>C & AG:</u> The Office of the Comptroller and Auditor General is the second agent of external administrative accountability. The activities of the Office impinged on senior staff in departments mainly in relation to the provision of the necessary documentation for the annual audit. In some cases, a staff member of the Office was based permanently in a department.

Contact with the C & AG's office was largely confined to those senior civil servants or sections involved in the expenditure of monies. As Table 3.3 shows, about 30 per cent of all those interviewed saw the Office as a significant agent of accountability. It was marginally more important for assistant secretaries than for any other grade, but generally it was of most importance for officers with financial responsibilities and, among departments, for the largest spending departments. The Office was

Table 3.3 Senior Civil Servants' Perceptions of the Degree of Importance of the Office of the Comptroller and Auditor General for his/her Accountability, by Grade.

Level of Importance	Heads of Departments	Deputy/ Assistant Secretaries	Principal Officers	Total
High	3 (14%)	-	1 (3%)	4 (5%)
Moderate	2 (9%)	10 (31%)	8 (28%)	20 (24%)
Low	14 (63%)	9 (29%)	4 (13%)	27 (32%)
No	-	10 (31%)	13 (43%)	23 (27%)
No answer	3 (14%)	3 (9%)	4 (13%)	10 (12%)
N	22	32	30	84

perceived to be concerned largely with financial regularity and compliance. Only about 10 per cent of those interviewed believed that the role played by the C & AG in recent years had broadened --- embracing wider aspects of departmental performance, such as value for money, and issues related to efficiency. A number of respondents did point out, however, that procedures for the C & AG review were so well-known as to have become institutionalised.

(iii) The (former) Department of the Public Service: The final agent of external administrative accountability at the time of study was the now defunct Department of the Public Service. Other departments were required to report with an agreed frequency to the Department of the Public Service on the implementation of the management system as set out in the White Paper, Serving the Country Better. The details of these procedures will be outlined in the next chapter.

Apart from reporting on White Paper-related developments, line departments also submitted information to the Department of the Public Service on staffing levels, pay and related personnel issues and management systems. Since such reporting requirements generally were carried out by one section within the department, respondents felt that they did not constitute an active form of accountability for individual staff members.

3.4.3 Internal Parliamentary Accountability

This type of accountability was effected by either the minister, the minister(s) of state or both. Again, there was a good deal of variation in how accountability to the minister was exercised, depending on the operating style and interests of individual ministers.

Accountability to the minister was effected in three principal ways, in descending order of frequency:
- formal meetings
- informal meetings or briefing sessions
- written reports and submission of requested work (e.g., speeches, briefing reports).

The majority of departmental secretaries and heads of offices and commissions had regular meetings with their minister (and, less often, minister of state) at the time of the study. Informal discussions with the minister were also quite common. Written reports were less widespread.

3.4.4 External Parliamentary Accountability

Four agents of external parliamentary accountability were identified: Committee of Public Accounts, Committee on Public Expenditure, the Office of the Ombudsman, and parliamentary representatives, mainly through parliamentary questions.

(i) Committee of Public Accounts: The Committee of Public Accounts bases its review largely on the report of the C & AG, and calls the accounting officers as witnesses. The evidence from the study is that this Committee was a significant form of accountability for the secretaries/heads but had only a minimal influence on the work of deputy or assistant secretaries and principal officers.

(ii) Committee on Public Expenditure: The Committee on Public Expenditure was generally seen by respondents to be of greater significance than the Committee of Public Accounts because its brief is broader and its operation less institutionalised. The operation and impact of this Committee is the central focus of Chapter Five.

(iii) Office of the Ombudsman: Although the Office of the Ombudsman is not technically an instrument of parliamentary accountability, since it reports to the Dail, it can be classified as such. The operation and impact of this Office will be outlined in Chapter Six.

(iv) Parliamentary Representatives: Parliamentary representatives effect accountability from civil servants mainly through parliamentary questions (PQs). The volume of PQs varied widely across and within departments; not unexpectedly, most were received by officers who are responsible for service delivery to the public. It is interesting to consider senior civil servants' evaluations of the impact of PQs on their workload. PQs had an impact

Table 3.4   Senior Civil Servants' Evaluations of the Effect of Parliamentary Questions on his/ her Workload, by Grade

Level of Effect	Heads of Departments	Deputy/ Assistant Secretaries	Principal Officers	Total
High	8 (36%)	10 (31%)	7 (23%)	25 (30%)
Moderate	3 (14%)	5 (16%)	7 (23%)	15 (18%)
Low	7 (32%)	12 (38%)	10 (33%)	29 (34%)
No effect	1 (4%)	1 (3%)	1 (3%)	3 (4%)
No answer	3 (14%)	4 (12%)	5 (18%)	12 (14%)
N	22	32	30	84

on the workload of almost half of all respondents. Those departments/individuals engaged in service delivery to the public had the highest volume of PQs. Many senior civil servants commented that the new rota system for PQs had substantially facilitated the department's capacity to integrate PQs into their daily workloads. The work of only 4 per cent of respondents was unaffected by PQs.

3.5 Changing Accountability

The recent debates about accountability seem to have led to practical changes in that half of the senior civil servants who were interviewed had experienced a change in their accountability in recent years (Table 3.5). Deputy or assistant secretaries and principal officers experienced the most change.

Table 3.5   Senior Civil Servants' Perceptions of whether Their Accountability had Changed in the Recent Past, by Grade

Change	Heads of Departments	Deputy/ Assistant Secretaries	Principal Officers	Total
Yes	7 (32%)	17 (53%)	17 (57%)	41 (49%)
No	14 (64%)	14 (44%)	12 (40%)	40 (47%)
No answer	1 (4%)	1 (3%)	1 (3%)	3 (4%)
N	22	32	30	84

What had been the major sources of change?

The implementation of the management system that was
set out in the White Paper, Serving the Country
Better, was the single most widely perceived source
of change in overall accountability (Table 3.6). The
increased use of Select Dáil/Oireachtas committees of
enquiry, and especially the Committee on Public
Expenditure, was also seen to be a significant source
of change. The third agent of change mentioned was
the increased interest of the media and the public
generally in the operation of the civil service. The
operation and effects of the relevant White Paper
proposals and those of the Committee on Public
Expenditure, along with the Office of the Ombudsman,
will be explored in greater detail in subsequent
chapters.

The significance of the different sources of change
varied for different grades: for heads of
departments, deputy and assistant secretaries, the
increased use of Dáil/Oireachtas Committees had been
the most important source of change, whereas for
principal officers the White Paper-related
developments were the most significant.

Table 3.6   Senior Civil Servants' Views of how their
Accountability had Changed in the Recent
Past, by Grade*

Source of Change	Heads of Departments	Deputy/ Assistant Secretaries	Principal Officers	Total
White Paper-related changes	1 (14%)	3 (18%)	7 (40%)	12 (29%)
Increased use of Dáil/ Oireachtas Committees	3 (44%)	4 (23%)	3 (18%)	10 (24%)
More informed public/media	1 (14%)	4 (23%)	2 (12%)	6 (15%)
Changes in reporting procedures to Dept. of Finance	-	2 (12%)	2 (12%)	4 (10%)
General Cutbacks	1 (14%)	2 (12%)	1 (6%)	4 (10%)
Increased Ministerial & Cabinet involvement in executive matters	1 (14%)	1 (6%)	1 (6%)	3 (7%)
No answer	-	1 (6%)	1 (6%)	2 (5%)
N	7	17	17	41

*   Based on those who believed that their accountability
    had changed in recent years.

3.6 Perceived Effectiveness of Existing Practices

Only about a third of all those interviewed considered existing accountability practices to be satisfactory. Over half the respondents could pinpoint particular shortcomings in existing procedures. The following table sets these out:

Table 3.7   Principal Perceived Shortcomings of Existing Accountability Procedures, by Grade*

Shortcomings	Heads of Departments	Deputy/ Assistant Secretaries	Principal Officers	Total
Internal administrative accountability inadequate	1 (10%)	7 (39%)	7 (43%)	15 (34%)
Role of minister unclear	4 (40%)	6 (33%)	3 (19%)	13 (30%)
Procedures inadequate	4 (40%)	5 (28%)	3 (19%)	12 (27%)
Overlap in different channels of accountability	1 (10%)	–	3 (19%)	4 (9%)
N	10	18	16	44

* Based on those who could identify shortcomings.

Three main shortcomings were identified. They are, in descending order of importance:

- internal administrative or managerial
  accountability, in the sense of being held to
  account for performance within the department,
  is inadequately effected
- the role of the minister in relation to the
  other agents of accountability is unclear
- the procedures for effecting accountability are
  inadequate, viz. inadequate information
  systems, no comprehensive reporting mechanisms.

The relative priority of each of the three varied for
the different grades. Among secretaries and heads of
offices or commissions, the lack of clarity in the
role of the minister and the inadequate reporting
mechanisms and procedures were predominant. Deputy
and assistant secretaries, while concerned about the
role of the minister, were most concerned about the
inadequacies in internal administrative
accountability procedures. This was also the
predominant concern among principal officers.

In summary, parliamentary and administrative
accountability were regarded as the most important
forms of accountability. The sources of and channels
through which accountability was exercised vary
considerably, grade being an important

differentiating factor. There was a good deal of
interdepartmental variation as well. The evidence
from senior civil servants confirmed that change was
underway. Only a third of those who were interviewed
felt that existing accountability mechanisms were
effective at the time of study.

Chapter Four

SENIOR CIVIL SERVANTS' PERCEPTIONS OF THE IMPLEMENTATION AND EFFECTS OF THE WHITE PAPER, **SERVING THE COUNTRY BETTER**

4.1 Introduction

This chapter outlines how internal accountability systems were seen to have been affected by the implementation of the management-related reforms in the White Paper, Serving the County Better. Since fieldwork for the study was concluded in March 1986, only the preliminary phase of the White Paper's implementation was investigated. This chapter first sets out the stages that departments had reached in implementing the White Paper's reforms by the end of January 1986. It then goes on to examine respondents' perceptions of the impact of the reforms on their own and their department's efficiency and effectiveness. Finally, the reactions of the senior civil servants to the relevant White Paper reforms is briefly explored.

4.2 Progress and Perceived Effects of the White Paper

The management reforms that were set out in the White Paper were directed at two levels: departmental and individual senior manager.

4.2.1 Perceived Impact at Departmental Level

The majority of those interviewed believed that the White Paper had made an impact on their department. Replies suggested that, before the first implementation phase of the White Paper, internal accountability practices in most departments were largely informal and ad hoc. Little by way of a standardised system of internal accountability seems to have existed. This was reportedly beginning to change at the time of the present study.

While the implementation of the White Paper had not led to a standardised accountable management system, it was generally seen to have provided:
- an impetus to develop, record and implement departmental and individual objectives, and
- a standardised guide or framework for these activites.

At the time of the study, departments were about to formalise what often up to then had been informal practice.

An attempt was made to assess the situation in each department regarding the implementation of the White Paper's system of managerial accountability. While this information proved rather difficult to obtain, it was possible to find out the activities that departments had engaged in by January 1986 to implement the White Paper's system of managerial accountability.

Three main steps or stages were involved in implementing the new system. These are illustrated in Table 4.1, along with the progress so far achieved.

Table 4.1   Perceived Departmental Progress by January 1986 in Implementing the Management System Set Out in the White Paper*

Stages/Activities	% of Departments/Offices/ Commissions known to have undertaken this Activity
Statement of departmental goals	74%
Identification and costing of results	32%
Monitoring of performance	13%

* These data must be treated cautiously since they were compiled on the basis of reports from a number of individuals within the relevant departments.

Most departments, offices and commissions reportedly had finalised by January 1986 an agreed statement of

departmental goals and objectives. This usually was
prepared through the MAC, where it existed, or by the
secretary and assistant secretaries in those
departments, offices or commissions that did not have
an operational MAC. Respondents in five departments
believed that the implementation of the White Paper
had led to the establishment or reactivation of the
MAC in their departments.

There was quite a large gap, however, between the
first and second stages of implementation: at the
time of study, only 32 per cent of departments,
offices or commissions had completed the second stage
of identifying and costing results. Finally, by
January 1986 only 13 per cent of departments had
begun to monitor overall performance.

The White Paper was not the motivating factor in all
cases. Two departments already had instituted a
system resembling that set forth in the White Paper
and a number of others had begun to spell out their
objectives independently of the White Paper.
However, most of those interviewed acknowledged that
the White Paper, and in particular the stipulation
that the departments should report to the former
Department of the Public Service on progress achieved

by December 1985, had been a significant spur to
action.

Departments generally took advantage of the leeway
and flexibility in the White Paper, with the result
that departmental interpretations of the concept of
accountable management and the activities needed to
bring it about varied considerably. Some departments
carried out only a partial review --- reviewing
activities and structures for their capacity to stay
within budget --- whereas others had begun to
appraise departmental efficiency and effectiveness.
As regards practices as a whole, two areas appeared
to be problematic:

- setting goals and developing monitoring systems
  in sections and departments that were engaged in
  policy formulation
- interlinking departmental goals and targets with
  those of individual managers.

4.2.2 Perceived Impact at the Individual Level of
Operation

Change was more difficult to discern at this level.
Perceptions about whether the implementation of the
management system in the White Paper had affected the
operations of individual civil servants varied by

grade and across departments. Only about 20 per cent
of respondents said that their operations had changed
as a result of the White Paper. The pursuit of
specified goals was the main type of change that had
occurred. The work of heads of departments was least
likely to have been influenced by the implementation
of the White Paper, whereas the work of assistant
secretaries was most affected --- the responsibility
for preparing and undertaking the necessary
activities to implement the White Paper resided
usually at this level. The work of principal
officers was also affected, but only in those five
departments that at the time of study had devolved
accountability to this grade level.

4.2.3 <u>Perceived Impact of the White Paper on Efficiency</u>
Increased efficiency is a central, if indirect,
objective of the White Paper. Sixty per cent of
those who were interviewed said that efficiency was
an integral part of their operations (Table 4.2).
For a further 20 per cent of the study population,
efficiency, while a consideration, was not an active
pursuit. About 16 per cent of the respondents viewed
efficiency as unimportant or as irrelevant to their
operations. The majority of these were involved in
policy formulation.

Perceptions	Heads of Departments	Deputy/ Assistant Secretaries	Principal Officers	Total
Integral to operations	14 (63%)	19 (59%)	18 (60%)	51 (61%)
Important but incidental to operations	6 (27%)	7 (22%)	4 (13%)	17 (20%)
Not relevant	–	4 (13%)	5 (17%)	9 (11%)
Not important	1 (5%)	2 (6%)	1 (3%)	4 (5%)
No answer	1 (5%)	–	2 (7%)	3 (3%)
N	22	32	30	84

Two main points are notable about efficiency. First,
it was generally defined in terms of the costs
incurred: efficiency tended to be interpreted as
making do with less rather than as part of a
comparison between inputs and outputs. Second, the
pursuit of efficiency was centred on particular
activities. The annual compilation of the
departmental estimates was reportedly a major
occasion for reviewing departmental efficiency. The
return of monthly expenditure data to the Department
of Finance also led departments to appraise their

efficiency: here again efficiency tended to be equated with staying within budget. In all, efficiency reviews in their own right were not widespread across departments at the time of study.

The implementation of the White Paper was said to be too recent to have made a major impact on departmental efficiency at the time of study. However, the public service embargo on recruitment was widely mentioned as having improved the use of resources. The general reduction in available expenditure was also a significant force for change. Being compelled to produce (approximately) the same service with less staff had, it was claimed, led to a more considered use of staff and other resources.

The embargo on recruitment and general cuts in expenditure have not been without their costs. Over the course of the embargo, the less visible and pressing work had reportedly not been processed as before. It was felt that the consequences of this would become apparent in the long-term since such work, despite its lower visibility, may be just as essential to departmental efficiency.

Computerisation and a more widespread use of
technology were highlighted as important in the
pursuit of efficiency. Relatedly, adequate
management information systems were seen as vital,
and existing internal information systems were
thought to be in need of improvement. A second
problem mentioned by senior civil servants in regard
to efficiency was the difficulty of measuring
workload or work output, given the diversity of the
tasks involved and, in many cases, their
unspecifiable nature.

4.2.4 <u>Perceived Impact of the White Paper on Effectiveness</u>
Effectiveness --- setting objectives and monitoring
progress towards achieving them --- was a relatively
less widespread issue among senior civil servants
than was efficiency at the time of study. In
general, effectiveness was integral to the operations
of about a third of the senior civil servants
interviewed, while a further 6 per cent said that
they had begun to consider effectiveness as part of
their everyday operation (Table 4.3). Principal
officers expressed most interest in effectiveness.

In contrast, just about a third of those who were
interviewed considered effectiveness to be either

Table 4.3   Senior Civil Servants' Perceptions of
             the Importance of Effectiveness, by Grade

Perceptions	Heads of Departments	Deputy/ Assistant Secretaries	Principal Officers	Total
Integral to operations	4 (18%)	8 (24%)	12 (40%)	24 (29%)
Important but incidental to operations	6 (27%)	5 (16%)	8 (27%)	19 (23%)
Beginning to pursue it	2 (9%)	3 (9%)	1 (3%)	6 (6%)
Hope to start	1 (5%)	4 (13%)	-	5 (6%)
Not important	4 (18%)	5 (16%)	6 (20%)	15 (18%)
Not relevant	5 (23%)	5 (16%)	2 (7%)	12 (14%)
No answer	-	2 (6%)	1 (3%)	3 (4%)
N	22	32	30	84

unimportant or irrelevant for them. These
individuals were drawn from a range of departments,
but they were mostly officers whose function is set
down by statute or regulation or whose operation is
dependent on bodies or agencies external to the
department, e.g., state-sponsored bodies.

The White Paper was generally acknowledged as likely
to be a significant influence towards improved
departmental effectiveness. Setting out objectives,

devising a framework whereby progress is to be measured and actually monitoring performance --- all activities required by the White Paper --- were acknowledged as being central to effectiveness.

The evidence suggests that certain factors complicate the monitoring of effectiveness in the civil service. It requires clear-cut objectives and a capacity to assess the progress that has been achieved. Certain tasks within the civil service meet neither of these criteria; policy formulation, for example, where it is difficult to set objectives and assess achievements. A second obstacle to the pursuit of effectiveness in the civil service is the fact that goals are frequently set outside the department and are often immutable. Each of these factors emphasises the special nature of public sector effectiveness and poses a challenge to develop an application of effectiveness that is fully realisable in departments of state.

4.3 Senior Civil Servants' Attitudes to the Management System Set Out in the White Paper

Respondents' attitudes to the management system that was set out in the White Paper are outlined in Table 4.4.

Table 4.4   Senior Civil Servants' Attitudes to the
             Accountable Management System Set Out in
             the White Paper, by Grade

Attitudes	Heads of Departments	Deputy/ Assistant Secretaries	Principal Officers	Total
Unreservedly favourable	7 (32%)	15 (47%)	10 (33%)	32 (38%)
Favourable with reservations	5 (23%)	11 (34%)	9 (30%)	25 (30%)
Unfavourable	10 (45%)	5 (16%)	7 (23%)	22 (26%)
Don't know/ no answer	–	1 (3%)	4 (14%)	5 (6%)
N	22	32	30	84

A majority of the senior civil servants who were
interviewed was generally favourable towards the
management system proposed in the White Paper.
Thirty-eight per cent regarded it favourably without
qualification, and a further 30 per cent welcomed it
with some reservations. About a quarter of those
interviewed regarded the management system
unfavourably.

When particular grades are taken into account,
significant differences become apparent.
Departmental secretaries and heads of offices or
commissions were least favourable to the management

system that was set out in the White Paper: almost half responded negatively to it. Deputy and assistant secretaries were most favourably disposed to it.

4.3.1 Perceived Benefits

Senior civil servants identified a number of benefits attaching to the White Paper:

- by focusing on the department as a unit, it facilitated the development of corporate consciousness, and clarified departmental objectives and the contribution of individual managers
- it made a commitment to greater delegation and set out to achieve this in a structured way
- frequently it formalised what was happening in an informal way
- it allowed departments and senior civil servants a necessary degree of autonomy and flexibility in setting up new systems or altering existing ones.

4.3.2 Reservations Expressed

Table 4.5 sets out the reservations that were expressed about the White Paper.

Table 4.5 Senior Civil Servants' Reservations about the Management System Set Out in the White Paper, by Grade*

Reservations	Heads of Departments	Deputy/ Assistant Secretaries	Principal Officers	Total
No legislative change re. ministerial position	5 (33%)	7 (43%)	4 (25%)	16 (35%)
Not enough authority/ control delegated to civil servants	5 (33%)	4 (25%)	4 (25%)	13 (29%)
Difficult to implement	3 (20%)	3 (19%)	4 (25%)	10 (19%)
Not new; what it sets out already in place	1 (7%)	2 (13%)	3 (19%)	6 (13%)
No answer	1 (7%)	-	1 (6%)	2 (4%)
N	15	16	16	47

* Based on those who expressed reservations about, or reacted negatively to, the White Paper's management-related reforms.

Of most concern if the system of accountable management set out in the White Paper is to be truly workable was the need for legislative change in the position of the minister as the 'corporation sole'. It was acknowledged that the White Paper's stated intention to effect 'legal changes' was too vague. These respondents pointed out that the relationship

with the minister was of critical importance for
senior civil servants but was typically informal and
highly dependent on interpersonal factors. They were
concerned that the implementation of the new
management system would upset the balance of the
relationship without giving them any compensating
authority.

The second most widespread source of concern is a
related one --- that senior civil servants will be
held accountable without having a commensurate level
of authority, i.e., they will be held accountable for
activities over which they have no control. There is
a fear that, in the absence of such control being
granted to senior civil servants, accountability
systems will operate only to apportion blame when
something goes amiss.

Potential implementation problems were also a source
of concern. A number of points were made here.
First was the fear that implementing the new system
would place additional pressures on departments,
mainly by creating extra work. Second, some senior
civil servants perceived a disjunction between the
financial and general management systems and feared
that such a lack of integration may result in

procedures being duplicated and lead to long-term
inefficiency. The frequent reporting requirements to
(at that time) two central departments was regarded
as being counter to true accountability and
delegation. Furthermore, it was feared that
departments could become 'report-bound', and that the
practice of accountability would become an end in
itself. A related concern was that the proposed
changes would act to slow up work rather than to
expedite the processing of work.

In general, implementation of the White Paper was at
an early stage when the study was carried out.
Although most departments, offices and commissions
had set out specific goals, neither departmental
structures nor individual or departmental operations
were found to have changed significantly.

Chapter Five

SENIOR CIVIL SERVANTS' PERCEPTIONS OF THE WORK OF THE COMMITTEE ON PUBLIC EXPENDITURE

5.1 Introduction

This chapter outlines senior civil servants' perceptions of the work of the Committee on Public Expenditure up to January 1986. The initial contacts with the Committee are first described, followed by the identified effects of the Committee's operation at the time of study. Finally, senior civil servants' perceptions of the benefits and disadvantages of the Committee are examined.

5.2 Initial Contacts with the Committee on Public Expenditure

The Committee was said to establish contact with departments of state in two main ways. First, all departments received copies of a very detailed questionnaire, on their management, efficiency and accountability practices, which was used by the Committee to obtain initial information on departmental operations. Generally, this questionnaire was completed at the highest level within departments. Secondly, about a quarter of those interviewed, comprising staff members of all but four departments, offices or commissions, had appeared personally before the Committee.

Among these were represented relatively even proportions of the five grades studied. The fact that only five departmental secretaries or heads of offices or commissions had appeared personally as witnesses illustrates the Committee's practice of seeking information directly from the officer in charge of the area of work that is relevant to its enquiries.

The Committee has taken an interest in a wide range of topics. Some of the respondents had a brief, single appearance, typically when a topic was being reviewed for its suitability for more detailed enquiry. More sustained contact with the Committee was likely to occur as part of its comprehensive reviews. At the time of study, a departmental review had been carried out in the former Department of the Public Service and was proceeding in the then Department of Industry, Trade, Commerce and Tourism.

Other departments reporting a good deal of contact
with the Committee at the time of the study were
Social Welfare, Labour, Health and the Office of
Public Works.

5.3 Approach Taken to the Committee on Public Expenditure

The approach adopted to an appearance before the
Committee varied. While all departments took the
appearance seriously, some adopted and prepared in
advance a corporate approach, devoting more time and
planning to their appearance(s) than other
departments. Concern was expressed about the
usefulness of the guidelines for such appearances
issued by the former Department of the Public
Service. Some senior civil servants felt that to
refuse to reply to a policy-relevant question, as the
guidelines recommend, placed them in a difficult
position and made them appear unhelpful.

Personal appearances before this and other Dáil/
Oireachtas Committees require particular presentation
skills that are new to many senior civil servants.
The need to develop such skills is likely to grow in
the civil service in line with the increased use of
Select Oireachtas Committees and general moves to

heighten the public visibility of civil servants. At
the time of study, heads of departments expressed a
concern about the latter. In their view, the
principal officer grade, and that of assistant
secretary to a lesser extent, would benefit
considerably from relevant skill development
courses. This was felt to be an identifiable gap in
training provisions for civil servants.

5.4 Some Effects of the Committee on Public Expenditure

Since the scale of the Committee's investigations is
wide-ranging, its potential impact on departments and
senior civil servants is very broad. When
investigating the Committee's perceived outcome,
three main dimensions were explored: departmental
structures, operations and attitudes.

5.4.1 Structural Effects

Only one respondent could identify a structural
change resulting from an enquiry by or an appearance
before the Committee on Public Expenditure. In this
case, the Committee recommended structural
reorganisation. This was underway at the time of
study.

5.4.2 Operational Effects

The Committee had had a greater effect on the operation of the senior civil service. Forty per cent of those who were interviewed said that their work had been affected in some way by the Committee on Public Expenditure. These worked in a range of departments and, as Table 5.1 shows, were distributed relatively evenly among the top grades studied.

Table 5.1　Senior Civil Servants' Perceptions of whether their Operations had been Affected by the Committee on Public Expenditure

Operations Affected	Heads of Departments	Deputy/ Assistant Secretaries	Principal Officers	Total
Yes	9 (41%)	11 (34%)	13 (43%)	33 (39%)
No	13 (59%)	21 (66%)	17 (57%)	51 (61%)
N	22	32	30	84

The Committee's effect was not limited to those who had appeared personally before it; in fact, about half of those who had been affected by it had not personally appeared before the Committee. However, an appearance before the Committee was quite likely to have an effect: 68 per cent of those in the study population who had appeared before it said that their operations had changed in some way as a result of the appearance.

What was the nature of these changes?

Where the Committee was seen to have affected operations, its main impacts had been to increase caution in decision-making and to tighten controls (Table 5.2). While the Committee was said not

Table 5.2   Perceived Effect of the Committee on Public Expenditure on Respondent/Section, by Grade*

Type of Effect	Heads of Departments	Deputy/ Assistant Secretaries	Principal Officers	Total		
More cautious decision-making and better back-up information	3 (33%)	3 (27%)	7 (54%)	13	(40%)	
Makes one enforce regulations/ tighten controls	3 (33%)	4 (36%)	1 (8%)	8	(24%)	
Increased workload	1 (11%)	3 (27%)	–	4	(12%)	
Changes in the processing of work	2 (23%)	1 (10%)	1 (8%)	4	(12%)	
Leads to self/ section review	–	–	2 (15%)	2	(6%)	
More cost conscious	–	–	2 (15%)	2	(6%)	
N	9	11	13	33		

* Based on those who said that the Committee on Public Expenditure had affected their operations.

to have affected the content of decisions taken
within departments, it had led to more considered
decision-making and to the provision of better back-
up information to document and justify decisions.
'Carefulness' and 'caution' were frequently mentioned
in this context, and the provision of comprehensive
back-up information on decisions assumed greater
priority. This effect was most pronounced among
principal officers. A related impact had been the
more strict enforcement of regulations. About a
quarter of all those whose operations had been
affected by the Committee said that they were
enforcing regulations more strictly.

A less widespread effect identified for the Committee
was increased workloads: only 12 per cent of those
who had been affected reported this outcome. Changes
in the processing of work were similarly infrequent.

5.4.3 Attitudinal Effects

The Committee had had a slightly less significant
effect on the attitudes of senior civil servants:
about a third of those interviewed said that their
attitudes had been changed in some way by the
Committee. Among these, it had provoked a greater
consciousness and awareness that the internal systems

of decision-making and management should stand up to external scrutiny. Furthermore, consciousness of cost reputedly had become a more active, although it was emphasised not a new, concern in decision-making. However, some individuals queried whether more cautious decision-making was better decision-making; there was a fear that work would be slowed down as a result.

Having documented the perceived impact of the Committee on the respondents' own area of operation, what is their view of the scale of its impact throughout the civil service?

In general, the Committee was perceived to have had quite a limited impact and to have affected only those departments with which it had had continuing contact. Only a third of respondents believed that the Committee had had a significant impact on the civil service generally. Two main types of impact were identified: an increased consciousness of money and the need to control expenditure; and a decrease in morale. The view was expressed that the potential impact of the Committee had been diluted by the diversity of its investigations and by the manner in which it had chosen to pursue its activities.

5.5 General Attitudes towards the Committee on Public Expenditure

Half of all the senior civil servants the Committee positively, 42 per cent held generally negative attitudes towards the Committee, while 7 per cent were undecided (Table 5.3). Heads of departments

Table 5.3   Senior Civil Servants' General Attitudes Towards the Committee on Public Expenditure, by Grade

Attitude	Heads of Departments	Deputy/Assistant Secretaries	Principal Officers	Total
Generally positive	8 (36%)	16 (50%)	18 (60%)	42 (50%)
Generally Negative	11 (50%)	12 (38%)	12 (40%)	35 (42%)
Undecided	3 (14%)	3 (9%)	–	6 (7%)
No answer	–	1 (3%)	–	1 (1%)
N	22	32	30	84

were more negative in their attitudes than either deputy/assistant secretaries or principal officers. A majority of those who had appeared before the Committee regarded it positively. Specific benefits and shortcomings were seen to attach to the Committee.

5.5.1 Perceived Benefits

The main perceived benefit of the Committee on Public Expenditure was that it fulfilled a need. There were three distinct elements to this. First is the perceived need for an <u>overview</u> of effectiveness to be undertaken; second, there is an expressed need for <u>external</u> scrutiny; third, the <u>deterrent</u> or <u>preventive</u> aspects of the Committee's operation were seen to fulfil a need. Nearly 60 per cent of the study population cited one of these three outcomes as a primary benefit of the Committee on Public Expenditure (Table 5.4). Another, although much less widely perceived, benefit of the Committee was that it increased the flow of information to the public.

Table 5.4 also shows that a small group of respondents (14 per cent), while approving of the Committee's existence, felt that its operation was poor. A further 17 per cent of the study population failed to identify any benefits of the Committee.

What shortcomings were seen to exist?

5.5.2 Perceived Shortcomings

There were three main sources of comment here (Table

Table 5.4   Perceived Benefits of the Committee on Public
             Expenditure, by Grade

Benefits	Heads of Departments	Deputy/ Assistant Secretaries	Principal Officers	Total
Overview/check on effectiveness	7 (32%)	9 (28%)	11 (36%)	27 (32%)
External Scrutiny	3 (14%)	4 (12%)	5 (17%)	12 (14%)
Theoretically it is good but its operation is poor	2 (9%)	7 (22%)	3 (10%)	12 (14%)
A deterrent/ reduces waste	2 (9%)	6 (19%)	2 (7%)	10 (12%)
Increases information to the public	2 (9%)	–	3 (10%)	5 (6%)
No benefits	4 (18%)	5 (16%)	5 (17%)	14 (17%)
No answer	2 (9%)	1 (3%)	1 (3%)	4 (5%)
N	22	32	30	84

5.5).   They are, in descending order of importance to

the respondents:

- approach and operation of the Committee

- effects on staff morale

- role and structure.

Table 5.5   Perceived Shortcomings of the Committee on Public Expenditure, by Grade

Shortcomings	Heads of Departments	Deputy/ Assistant Secretaries	Principal Officers	Total
Approach and Operation				
Presence of the press	5 (23%)	8 (25%)	8 (26%)	21 (25%)
Confrontational approach	7 (31%)	2 (7%)	2 (7%)	11 (13%)
Partial review	2 (9%)	2 (7%)	3 (10%)	7 (8%)
Staff Morale				
Reduced morale and public confidence	2 (9%)	11 (34%)	5 (17%)	18 (22%)
Role and Structure				
Role unclear/ limited power	4 (18%)	3 (9%)	3 (10%)	10 (12%)
Overlap with Pac	1 (5%)	3 (9%)	3 (10%)	7 (8%)
No shortcomings	1 (5%)	3 (9%)	4 (13%)	8 (10%)
No answer	-	-	2 (7%)	2 (2%)
N	22	32	30	84

(a) **The Approach and Operation of the Committee:** Three main concerns were expressed about the Committee's approach and operation. The most widespread was the presence of the media and the perceived tendency of members to seek publicity through the Committee

for their own activities and interests. The presence
of the press at meetings was identified as a key
determinant of how the Committee conducts its
interrogations. Furthermore, it was seen by some
senior civil servants to influence the Committee's
choice of subject matter and to encourage members to
treat quite complex matters or subjects in a manner
that is conducive to media reporting.

The second operational issue that was raised referred
to the approach adopted by some members of the
Committee towards witnesses. A certain level of
disappointment was expressed, especially by heads of
departments, about the perceived confrontational
approach towards civil servants taken by some members
of the Committee. Relatedly, some concern was
expressed about the position of the senior civil
servant when giving evidence to the Committee. The
absence of privilege for the witness was regretted.

The third operational concern was the Committee's
capacity and willingness to take an overview of
departmental spending. As it had operated up to the
time of study, the Committee was seen to have taken a
greater interest in the minutiae of expenditure or
once-off items of former capital expenditure, than

the broader pattern of spending as it related to departmental objectives.

(b) Effects on Staff Morale: The main expressed concern here was that the operation of the Committee would indirectly act to lower morale in the civil service. This could happen in two ways. First, since the task of the Committee leads it to focus on specific problems, it necessarily draws attention to the negative aspects of civil service operations, thereby decreasing morale among staff. Secondly, staff morale is affected by the level of public confidence in the civil service, which was felt to have fallen since the Committee came into being. This was a particular concern among deputy and assistant secretaries.

(c) Role and Structure: There were two main concerns here. First, the Committee's role was felt by some respondents to have been unclear at the time of study. While these recognised that the Committee was still in the process of evolving, doubts were expressed about whether the Committee was pursuing a consistent set of objectives. The other main problems related to the perceived overlap between the Committee's operation and that of the Committee of

Public Accounts. There was some support for a merging of the two Committees.

Summarising, in its first two-and-a-half years the Committee on Public Expenditure has had an impact at two levels:

- at the <u>operational</u> level, it has led to more cautious decision making and to the compilation of more extensive back-up information to justify decisions

- at the <u>attitudinal</u> level, it has made senior civil servants more conscious of external scrutiny.

Chapter Six

SENIOR CIVIL SERVANTS' PERCEPTIONS

OF THE OFFICE OF THE OMBUDSMAN

6.1 Introduction

The Office of the Ombudsman is a very recent
institution in Ireland, having been set up in
January 1984. To open, this chapter briefly
describes the operation of the Office. Senior civil
servants' experience of and views on the influence of
the Office on departmental structures and operations
are then outlined. The reactions and attitudes of
senior civil servants to the Office will also be
explored.

6.2 The Operation of the Office during 1984 and 1985

During its first year, the Office received 2,267
complaints, 68 per cent of which were within its
jurisdiction. Sixty-five per cent of the valid cases
received were completed within the year. The
majority of cases outside the Office's jurisdiction
related to personnel matters in the civil service.

Of those cases that were defined as completed, 39 per cent were resolved, 29 per cent were not upheld, assistance was provided in 15 per cent, and 17 per cent were discontinued or withdrawn. During its first year of operation, a number of government departments challenged the Office's authority on points of law: the Departments of Posts and Telegraphs, Education, and Social Welfare, along with Bord Telecom.(1) Action taken by the Office was upheld by legal opinion in all cases.

During 1985, the volume of complaints to the Office more than doubled to 5,496. A smaller proportion (12 per cent) than in the 1984 caseload was outside the Office's remit, reflecting perhaps the extension of its terms of reference. Fifteen per cent of valid complaints were withdrawn or discontinued in that year, a slight decrease over the 1984 figure.

According to international comparison, Ireland is characterised by a high rate of complaints from its citizens. In Britain, for example, the Parliamentary Commissioner for Administration received an average of 992 complaints a year between 1976 and 1978.(2) Although Britons may tend to underuse this grievance procedure, Irish levels of complaint are still high

when compared with the French use of the Mediateur,
which in the same period averaged 3,478 complaints a
year. The political representative filter, which
operates in both Britain and France, undoubtedly
depresses the level of complaint, but general
comparison suggests that the Irish level of use of
the Ombudsman mechanism is significantly higher than
the international norm.

Not unexpectedly perhaps, the larger service
delivery departments were the subject of the majority
of complaints. Of all complaints received in the
first year, the Department of Social Welfare alone
accounted for 48 per cent. This department, together
with the Office of the Revenue Commissioners and the
Department of Posts and Telegraphs, accounted for 80
per cent of all complaints received by the Office
during 1984. There appear to be a few sources of
persistent complaint: Old Age Pensions and the
averaging problem (i.e., the system of deciding
entitlement), Disability Benefit, Unemployment
Benefit and Assistance, tax relief and rebates, and
problems with telephone bills and accounts.

Similar patterns persisted during 1985, except that
the enlargement of the Office's jurisdiction had some

interesting outcomes. For instance, non-civil service complaints accounted for almost half of all valid complaints received by the Office during 1985. The statistics for 1985 again indicate that a few particular problems accounted for the majority of complaints. In that year, for example, problems with telephone accounts comprised over a quarter of all cases dealt with by the Office. Similarly, when the nature of complaints against departments is examined, particular schemes consistently emerge as problematic.

6.3 Senior Civil Servants' Experience of the Office of the Ombudsman

Nineteen of the eighty-four respondents (23 per cent) had had personal contact with the Office: 18 per cent of heads of departments, 22 per cent of deputy or assistant secretaries and 27 per cent of principal officers. They were drawn from eight different departments or offices/ commissions, all except one of which is a major service department.

Respondents' experience confirms the Office's statistics in that departments' level of contact with the Office depended largely on the extent of their dealings with the public. In all, only two departments, Energy and the Taoiseach, were known to have received no queries from the Office at the time of study.

The number of queries and the extent of contact varied widely, as did the consequent impact on workloads. Most of the larger departments had appointed a liaison person, usually at principal officer grade, to deal with queries from the Office. However, official replies to queries from the Office were usually sanctioned at the assistant secretary level. Informal queries from the Office, of which there were many in the large service delivery departments, tended to be processed at a lower level, generally at HEO grade.

Most of those respondents who had had personal contact with the Office spoke highly of the approach taken by its staff. It was generally felt that the staff of the Office placed great emphasis on building up good relationships with departmental personnel. Informal contacts were said to be particularly significant in this regard. Only a small proportion of respondents expressed negative feelings about their contact with the Office.

6.4 The Office's Influence

The Office of the Ombudsman could not reasonably be
expected to have made a major influence on
departments at the time of study, given its newness
and the fact that its function does not relate
centrally to the operation and organisation of
departments. However, because it can query
administrative decisions on the basis of complaints
received, it is reasonable to expect the Office to
have some influence on senior civil servants.

Using the three-part framework of impact ---
structural, operational and attitudinal --- the data
suggested that the Office of the Ombudsman had made
only a limited impact. Not unexpectedly,
no structural effects on departments were identified
by respondents. Operationally, the Office was said
to have made two particular impacts:

- some changes in the processing of certain claims
  and in the determination of some entitlements
  for benefits in certain service delivery
  departments
- more careful record and file preparation in two
  departments.

Only those departments that had been in contact with the Office reported any operational effects.

The Office had had its most identifiable influence at an _attitudinal_ level. Staff were reported to be more conscious of an external scrutiny process and, consequently, to have adopted a more careful approach to decision-making. Realising that their decisions might be queried, they reported that they take greater care to ensure the interests of the citizen are fairly reflected in their decisions. Even though it was the most widespread one identified, this effect was still largely limited to the three or four departments or offices that had had most contact with the Office.

The Office's impact was seen to have been limited because the administrative system operates so fairly. The Ombudsman's own statistics lend some support to this: of all the cases completed in 1984, 46 per cent were either not upheld or were discontinued or withdrawn.(3) Some departments also pointed out that they had their own grievance or appeal systems.

6.5 General Attitudes to the Office of the Ombudsman

As Table 6.1 shows, senior civil servants were markedly receptive to the Office of the Ombudsman. Nearly three-quarters of those who were interviewed held generally positive attitudes to the Office; only 17 per cent viewed it negatively. Deputy and assistant secretaries held the most positive views of all.

Table 6.1   Senior Civil Servants' General Attitudes towards the Office of the Ombudsman, by Grade

Attitudes	Heads of Departments	Deputy/ Assistant Secretaries	Principal Officers	Total
Generally positive	14 (64%)	28 (88%)	19 (63%)	61 (73%)
Generally negative	5 (23%)	2 (6%)	8 (27%)	15 (17%)
Ambivalent	1 (4%)	-	2 (7%)	3 (4%)
No answer	2 (9%)	2 (6%)	1 (3%)	5 (6%)
N	22	32	30	84

6.5.1 Perceived Benefits of the Office

Most senior civil servants viewed the Office of the Ombudsman as being conducive to the interests of the public (Table 6.2). The Office was seen to fulfil a need, in that either the public is in need of an independent arbiter to deal with the

bureaucracy, or citizens have a right to query
administrative decisions and if necessary to have a
means of redressing them. Over half of those who
held positive attitudes to the Office saw that it
fulfilled either of these needs. A related view
expressed was that the Office helped to allay public

Table 6.2   Reasons why Senior Civil Servants held Positive
Attitudes towards the Office of the
Ombudsman, by Grade *

Reasons	Heads of Departments	Deputy/ Assistant Secretaries	Principal Officers	Total
Improves performance	2 (14%)	12 (43%)	4 (21%)	18 (30%)
Public need an independent arbiter	6 (43%)	5 (18%)	5 (26%)	16 (26%)
Public need redress access to decisions	4 (29%)	6 (21%)	5 (26%)	15 (25%)
Office has performed well to date	-	-	3 (16%)	3 (5%)
Creates better public understanding of civil service	-	2 (7%)	-	2 (3%)
No answer	2 (14%)	3 (11%)	2 (11%)	7 (11%)
N	14	28	19	61

* Based on those who hold positive attitudes to the
  Office of the Ombudsman.

fears about the civil service by demonstrating that (i) decisions can be queried and (ii) very few wrong decisions are taken.

The Office was also valued for its capacity to improve the performance of the civil service --- 30 per cent of positive attitudes were founded on this view. It was argued by these respondents that the existence and operation of the Office would lead, albeit indirectly, to better operations. Deputy and assistant secretaries, especially, valued this likely outcome.

The potential of the Office to act as an agent for change in matters that have remained unchanged because of political expediency was also mentioned. Relatedly, the Office was valued because it might help to introduce a more flexible approach to decision-making and to highlight that even in the civil service decisions often require individual judgments. The point made here was that investigations by the Ombudsman have shown that some decisions are not necessarily wrong, but that different ones could have been taken in particular instances.

6.5.2 Perceived Shortcomings of the Office

Notwithstanding these benefits, a small number of senior civil servants noted some reservations about the Office.

Basically, two sets of reservations about the Office were expressed. The first questioned whether it needs to exist --- that perhaps the public had been given an extra channel through which to complain. In this sense, the Office was seen to duplicate the function of PQs and personal representations by members of the Oireachtas. This view was supported by claims that the Office had had little effect on the volume of PQs and representations.

The second reservation related to the manner in which the Office of the Ombudsman had operated. A few respondents believed that the Office worked at too detailed a level, probing the wording of circulars, and so on, instead of investigating the equity of decisions. It was felt that the Office should look at the generality of a scheme or provision as much as its inclusions and exclusions.

In general, though, the senior civil servants who were interviewed viewed the existence and operation

of the Office of the Ombudsman very favourably. A
number of benefits were seen to attach to the Office,
especially the fact that it provides the public with
redress. It was also seen to be likely to improve
the performance of the civil sevice, although it must
be said that the Office had made only a limited
impact at the time of study.

REFERENCES

1. Office of the Ombudsman, First Report. Dublin :
   Stationery Office, 1985: 11-12.

2. W. Gwyn, 'The Ombudsman in Britain: A qualified
   success in Government reform,' Public
   Administration 60 (Summer 1982) : 185.

3. Office of the Ombudsman, First Report, op. cit., 58.

Chapter Seven

SUMMARY AND CONCLUSIONS

_____

7.1 Introduction

This chapter summarises the study's findings and
considers their main implications.

7.2 Accountability in Operation

It is clear from the study that there is no one type
of accountability in operation among the Irish senior
civil service. Nor is there just one channel for
effecting accountability. In practice, two systems
of accountability were identified, each with an
internal and external dimension. Figure 7.1 sets
these out, together with the main agents that exist
to effect them. They are as follows:

1. Internal administrative accountability -- effected
   in departments by the secretary or head and the
   management hierarchy

2. External administrative acountability -- effected
   by the Department of Finance (and formerly by the

Figure 7.1   Systems and Channels of Accountability for
              Senior Civil Servants

	Administrative System	Parliamentary System
Internal to Department	Secretary	Minister
	Hierarchy in department	Minister of State
External to Department	Department of Finance	Committee of Public Accounts
	Department of the Public Service*	Committee on Public Expenditure
	Office of the Comptroller and Auditor General**	Office of the Ombudsman
		Parliamentary Representatives

---

*   The former Department of the Public Service, now
    subsumed into the Department of Finance, operated
    as a separate department at the time this study
    was carried out.

** Technically, the Office of the Comptroller and
    Auditor General reports to the Dail but,
    operationally, it is part of the administrative
    rather than the parliamentary system.

Department of the Public Service) and by

the Office of the Comptroller and Auditor General

3. Internal parliamentary accountability -- effected

    within departments by the minister and minister(s)

    of state

4. <u>External parliamentary accountability</u> -- effected
   mainly by the Committee of Public Accounts and the
   Committee on Public Expenditure. The Office of
   the Ombudsman also affects the external
   accountability of the civil service.

   Parliamentary representatives, mainly through the
   use of parliamentary questions, also exact a form
   of accountability from the administration.

The perceived importance of each of these forms and
agents of accountability varies in practice; grade
has an important influence on which type of
accountability is seen to be primary.

Generally, internal parliamentary accountability,
especially that to the minister, and minister(s) of
state if relevant, was the most important form of
accountability for departmental secretaries and heads
of offices or commissions. Administrative
accountability was more important for the operation
of deputy and assistant secretaries and principal
officers, especially accountability within the
department.

Taking senior civil servants' perceptions of
accountability as a whole, four points were
striking:

- widespread interdepartmental variation
  characterises accountability practices: for
  instance, MACs, a key element in both internal
  management and accountability structures, were
  active in only seven departments at the time
  this study was carried out

- accountability practices are not clear-cut.
  Many procedures, both formal and informal, exist
  to effect accountability from the civil
  service.   Some overlap and duplicate one
  another.   In addition, it is questionable
  whether some of the procedures continue to
  effect accountability, given that their
  operation has become a routine

- practices were clearest in regard to financial
  accountability, for which many formal procedures
  exist within the civil service and parliamentary
  systems

- the extent to which senior civil servants were
  held accountable for administration and
  management within their department varied
  considerably at the time of study.   While
  internal administrative accountability was

generally informal, its extent depended largely on the individual style and priorities of the senior manager.

7.3 The Perceived Effects of Reforms on Senior Civil Servants' Accountability

This study investigated senior civil servants' perceptions of the effects of three particular developments: the implementation of the management framework that was set out in the White Paper, Serving the Country Better; the work of the Committee on Public Expenditure; the operation of the Office of the Ombudsman.

7.3.1 The White Paper, Serving the Country Better

The implementation of the management system that was set out in the White Paper, Serving the Country Better, was in its initial stages at the time of study: 74 per cent of departments, offices and commissions had set out corporate objectives; 30 per cent had identified and costed results; 13 per cent had the new management system up and going and were monitoring performance.

With regard to impact, structural change had occurred in five departments where it was reported that White

Paper-related developments had led to the establishment or reactivation of the MAC. Reflecting this departmental pattern, about a fifth of the senior civil servants in the study had experienced a change in their operations as a result of the White Paper. In general, the White Paper was perceived to be a significant motivator towards change, although change was already underway in a small number of departments.

For most respondents, efficiency --- a central objective of the White Paper --- was an important operational concern. They viewed efficiency largely in financial terms and saw it as being confined to routine activities (e.g., the preparation of the departmental estimates) rather than as a goal or objective for all activities. The White Paper had had little impact on respondents' pursuit of efficiency at the time of study, but the public service embargo on recruitment was felt to have been a major spur to increased departmental efficiency.

Effectiveness review appeared to be a less widespread activity in the Irish civil service at the time of study. Where such reviews did take place, their existence was attributed mainly to the White Paper.

The application of effectiveness, both as concept and practice, is problematic in some sectors of the civil service; in policy formulation, for instance, it is neither easy to set goals nor to assess whether they have been reached. Similarly, it is difficult to devise measures of effectiveness for an activity such as the servicing of the parliamentary system.

Notwithstanding these potential sources of difficulty, the implementation of the White Paper had already had a clear result at the time of study : it has helped to formalise and structure internal accountability procedures within a number of departments. Although specific procedures and their application varied widely at the time of study, all departments were engaged to some extent in appraising their own effectiveness and efficiency.

The senior civil servants who were interviewed were quite favourably disposed towards the management system that was set out in the White Paper. Heads of departments regarded it least favourably of all the grades studied. The benefits seen to attach to it mainly related to the development of corporate objectives and the commitment it made to delegation. Some concerns were also expressed: the need for legislative change in the position of the minister as the corporation sole; the need to grant senior civil servants greater control and authority, if they are to be held accountable; and some anticipated problems in implementing the new system.

In sum, the White Paper had had a significant effect in formalising systems through which the performance, efficiency and effectiveness of senior officers and their departments could be enhanced. Some variation existed, however, in the extent of commitment given to it and hence in its capacity to exert long-term change in the civil service.

7.3.2 The Committee on Public Expenditure

While the Committee was not reported to have had any effect on structures, forty per cent of senior civil servants said that some operational changes had resulted in their work as a result of the Committee's activities. Where it did have an effect, more cautious decision-making and better back-up information on decisions were reported, especially by principal officers. There was also some evidence that more strict enforcement of regulations had occurred as a result of the Committee's activities. Some respondents questioned the long-term benefits of

some of the changes to the way in which the civil
service operated, given that the avoidance of error
had assumed greater priority. A second perceived
impact of the Committee was on senior civil servants'
attitudes: about a third of those interviewed said
that they had become more conscious of the existence
and implications of external scrutiny procedures as a
result of the Committee's operation.

About half of all respondents held positive attitudes
towards the Committee. Generally, the Committee was
seen to fulfil a need for external scrutiny and
overview. Some problems were also identified,
however. Most problematic was the presence of the
press at meetings, which was seen to influence how
the Committee pursues its inquiries. The
relationship of senior civil servants to this and
other Committees emerged as an issue meriting
consideration. In sum, while the Committee on Public
Expenditure was not seen to have significantly
increased senior civil servants' accountability at
the time of study, its potential as a force for
future change was widely recognised.

'.3.3 The Office of the Ombudsman

Personal contact with the Office of the Ombudsman was

limited: only 23 per cent of respondents, drawn from
eight departments, had had personal contact with the
Office at the time of study. It is hardly
surprising, therefore, that the Office had had no
identifiable structural effects. It had affected
some operations (processing of claims and determining
some entitlements) in the larger service delivery
departments --- those that had been the major subject
of complaint to the Office. The Office was also seen
by a minority of respondents to have led to more
careful decision-making, and some respondents
reported an increased awareness of an external
scrutiny process. Attitudes to the Office and to its
staff were decidedly positive; most senior civil
servants readily acknowledged the right of the
citizen to query a decision that appears to be
adverse.

7.4 The State of Accountability Today

A central question runs through this study. Is the
civil service becoming more accountable? There is no
easy answer to this. It is certainly true that more
formal procedures now exist for effecting
accountability and that the controls exercised on the
senior civil servant from outside the department have
increased. Thus, there is greater parliamentary

scrutiny, through the Committee on Public Expenditure and other Committees; there is greater internal review of efficiency and effectiveness and more attempts to specify individual objectives and monitor performance, largely as a result of the implementation of the White Paper's system of accountable management; and there is an additional client appeal system in areas of direct service delivery, as a result of the Office of the Ombudsman. It is difficult to determine whether these significantly increased the accountability of the senior civil service. Taking them individually, the White Paper is likely to have the greatest influence on improving accountability because it has helped to set in place a system to account for performance and has provided a framework for formalising internal accountability. But since it was still in its early stages when this study was carried out, the full extent of its implementation and the degree of long-term commitment to it remain unknown.

While this study was carried out in late 1985 and early 19896 and, therefore, does not take account of consequent developments, it raises many issues that are of continuing importance in public management.

Six potential problems were highlighted.

- <u>the political/administrative interface:</u> Two main types of accountability, administrative and parliamentary, operate within the senior civil service, each of which has given rise to quite distinct reporting procedures. This in turn has meant the existence of parallel priorities within departments and within the civil service as a whole: parliamentary and administrative. Apart from the inefficiency caused by duplicated reporting procedures, there is the more fundamental question of which assumes priority for senior civil servants. In operational terms, the question becomes: who is the individual civil servant ultimately responsible to: the minister or the secretary? This is not a clear-cut either/or question. Throughout the study, departmental secretaries and heads of offices or commissions spoke of the difficulty of balancing parliamentary and administrative responsibilities. It seems to be difficult, if not nigh impossible, to legislate for this complex relationship, so dependent is it on the individual style of the ministerial incumbent. The role of the departmental head is to manage the political/administrative interface, which requires a delicate balancing of the two systems. The task of the departmental head is, therefore, considerably complex.

- the necessary variation in the work performed by senior civil servants: The difficulties of specifying objectives and developing monitoring systems are acute in certain parts of the civil service. Tasks involving policy formulation are a case in point. It is also difficult, however, to set targets and monitor progress in those areas of work that involve the servicing of the parliamentary system. This raises the question of whether it is either possible or desirable to treat the civil service as a unit. Certain tasks may require specific approaches, which differ from those required by others.

- the existing legal basis for accountability: This was a recurring concern, especially among heads of departments. At present the only legal accountability they have is as the departmental accounting officer. The central question here is whether senior civil servants are granted the authority or autonomy necessary to give full effect to their accountability. While they assume full responsibility for the operation and management of their departments, they are not

legally accountable for these activities. There
is a strong feeling among senior civil servants
that, if their accountability is to be formally
extended, it must be based on appropriate
legislative changes.

- the comprehensiveness of internal accountability
  systems within departments: Although the
  implementation of the White Paper was effecting
  change, some senior civil servants felt that
  they were not being held to account for their
  decisions and actions within the department at
  the time of study.

- accountability without responsibility: Some
  senior civil servants felt that they were being
  held accountable for decisions for which they
  were not responsible, i.e., those taken by a
  predecessor or the minister/minister of state.

- the costs of accountability: Increased
  acountability is not a costless exercise. Among
  the negative consequences of the three measures
  studied are slower, more cautious decision-
  making, more detailed record-keeping, and lower
  staff morale.

In conclusion, all attempts at reform in the Irish
civil service must be set in context. To focus on

one area is to ignore others. Accountability is just
one of many issues prevailing within the civil
service. At the end of the day, accountability is
not just a technical issue, such as better reporting
systems. It is the content of the reports --- the
performance --- that is critical. Better reporting
procedures do not automatically lead to better
performance. The focus of accountability should be
the need for continual improvement in performance,
not simply procedures themselves. Accountability for
what? should be the crucial question.

In the end, improved performance and improved
accountability depend on the extent to which people
accept them as legitimate goals, both within the
administration and within the parliamentary system.
The results of this study indicate that specific and
continued efforts may need to be made to generate and
sustain such commitment. The recognition that both
the administrative and parliamentary systems are
linked by a common goal --- improved public sector
performance and management --- is the key to
realising such commitment.

BIBLIOGRAPHY

A Better Way to Plan the Nation's Finances.   Dublin:
       Stationery Office, 1982.

Adamolekun, L., 'Accountability and control measures in
       public bureaucracies,' International Review of
       Administrative Sciences 40 (4:1974) : 307-321.

An Outline of Irish Financial Procedures. Dublin:
       Stationery Office, n.d.

Baker, W., 'Accountability, responsiveness and public
       sector productivity,' Canadian Public
       Administration 23 (1980) : 542-557.

Barrington, T., The Irish Administrative System Dublin:
       Institute of Public Administration, 1980.

Barrington, T., 'The task of the civil service in the
       1980s,' Seirbhis Phoibli 3 (1:1982) : 20-28.

Boland, J., 'Developing management skills in the civil
       service,' Seirbhís Phoiblí, 4 (Nollaig 1983):
       2-4.

Brooks, R., 'The Ombudsman and political control,' Local
       Government Studies July/August 1982.

Budget '87. Dublin: Stationery Office, 1987.

Building on Reality 1985-1987. Dublin: Stationery
       Office.

Cameron, D., 'Power and responsibility in the public
       service: Summary of discussions,' Canadian Public
       Administration 21 (3:1978) : 358-372.

Carman, R., 'Accountability of senior public servants to
       parliament and its committees,' Canadian Public
       Administration 27 (4:1984) : 542-555.

Chubb, B., The Government and Politics of Ireland.
       London: Longman, 1982.

Clarke, D., 'The citizen and the administration in France
       -- the Conseil d'Etat versus Ombudsman debate
       revisited,' Public Administration 62 (Summer
       1984) : 161-179.

Clarke, P., 'Performance evaluation of public sector programmes,' Administration 32 (3:1984) : 294-311.

Committee on Public Expenditure, Proposal to Establish a Centralised State Agency for Persons Registering for Employment or Training. Dublin: Stationery Office, May 1984.

Committee on Public Expenditure, First Annual Progress Report. Dublin: Stationery Office, October 1984.

Committee on Public Expenditure, Report on Office of Public Works. Dublin: Stationery Office, November 1984.

Committee on Public Expenditure, Review of Department of the Public Service. Dublin: Stationery Office, May 1985.

Committee on Public Expenditure, Control of Capital Projects. Dublin: Stationery Office, July 1985.

Comprehensive Public Expenditure Programmes. Dublin: Stationery Office, 1983.

Comprehensive Public Expenditure Programmes 1984. Dublin: Stationery Office, 1984.

Coombes, D., Representative Government and Economic Power. London : Heinemann, 1982.

Curran, D., 'An Ombudsman for Ireland,' Seirbhís Phoiblí 1 (2:1980): 10-14.

Currie, B., 'Framing targets for accountability,' Management Services in Government (August 1978) : 114-126.

Cutt, J., 'Accountability, efficiency and the Royal Commission on Australian Government administration,' Australian Journal of Public Administration 36 (December 1977) : 333-349.

Deloitte, Haskins and Sells, Public Sector Accounting and Research: Third Accounting and Research Symposium. London: Public Money General Series 3, 1984.

Dillon, M., 'Developments in public sector audit: How effective are efficiency audits?' Australian Journal of Public Administration 44 (3:1985): 247-269.

Dobell, A., 'Responsibility and the senior public service: Some reflections in summary,' Canadian Public Administration 27 (4:1984) : 617-627.

Dowling, J., 'Reflections on Minister John Boland's Louvain lecture,' Seirbhís Phoiblí 5 (2:1984) : 12-17.

Devlin, L. 'The management of change,' Seirbhis Phoibli 5 (2:1984) : 18-26.

Dunsire, A., Administration: The Work and the Science. London: Martin Robertson, 1973.

Dwivedi, O., 'Accountability of public servants: Recent developments in Canada,' Indian Journal of Public Administration 26 (3:1980) : 757-778.

Ennis,R., Accountability in Government Departments, Public Corporations and Public Companies. London: Lyon, Grant and Green, 1967.

Etzioni, A., 'Alternative conceptions of accountability: The example of health administration,' Public Administration Review (May/June 1975) : 279-286.

Finance, Department of, Guidelines for Financial Management. Pl. 299, November 1981.

Franks, C., 'Administrative accountability in Canada,' Indian Journal of Public Administration 29 (3:1983) : 690-713.

Friedman, B., The Quest for Accountability. Chicago: Public Administration Service, 1973.

Fulton Committee, The Civil Service Vol. 1. London: HMSO, 1968.

Gallhorn, W., Ombudsmen and Others: Citizens' Protectors in Nine Countries. Cambridge, Mass.: Harvard University Press, 1967.

Garrett, J., 'The accountable civil servant,' Management Today (November 1984) : 75-79

Gray, A., 'Codes of accountability and the presentation of an account: Towards a micro-administrative theory of public accountability,' <u>Public Administration Bulletin</u> 46 (December 1984) : 2-13.

Gray, A., and B. Jenkins, <u>Policy Analysis and Evaluation in British Government</u>. London: Royal Institute of Public Administration, 1983.

Gregory, R., and P. Hutchesson, <u>The Parliamentary Ombudsman</u>. London: Allen and Unwin, 1975.

Gwyn, W., 'The Ombudsman in Britain: A qualified success in government reform,' <u>Public Administration</u> 60 (Summer 1982) : 177-195.

Hally, D., 'Accountability and the public sector,' <u>Administration</u> 28 (2:1980) : 224-234.

Hogwood, B., <u>From Crisis to Complacency? Shaping Public Policy in Britain</u>. Oxford: Oxford University Press, 1987.

Hopwood, A., and C. Tomkins, (eds), <u>Issues in Public Sector Accounting</u>. London: Philip Allan, 1984.

House of Commons, Treasury and Civil Service Committee, <u>Efficiency and Effectiveness in the Civil Service</u>. Volume 1 Report. London: HMSO, 1982.

House of Commons, Treasury and Civil Service Committee, <u>Civil Servants and Ministers: Duties and Responsibilities</u>. London: HMSO, 1986.

Indian Journal of Public Administration, <u>Administrative Accountability</u>, July-September 1983 (29:3).

Johnson, N., <u>Parliament and Administration: The Estimates Committee 1945-65</u>. London: Allen and Unwin, 1966.

Joyce, L., <u>Administrators or Managers? An Exploratory Study of Public and Private Sector Decision Making</u>. Dublin: Institute of Public Administration, 1985.

Keeling, D., <u>Management in Government</u>. London: Allen and Unwin, 1972.

Kellner, P., and N. Crowther-Hunt, The Civil Servants.
    London: Mc Donald General Books, 1980.

Kelly, J., 'Administrative discretion,' Irish Jurist,
    N.S. 1966.

Kernaghan, K., 'Responsible public bureaucracy: A
    rationale and a framework for analysis,' Canadian
    Public Administration 16 (Autumn 1973) : 572-603.

Kiely, D., 'Ministers and departments -- The legal
    dimension: A view,' Seirbhís Phoiblí 7 (1:1986):
    7-15.

Laframboise, H., 'The responsibilities of a senior public
    servant: Organizations, profession and career,'
    Canadian Public Administration 27 (4:1984) : 592-
    600.

Langford, J., 'Responsibility in the senior public
    service: Marching to several drummers,' Canadian
    Public Administration 27 (4:1984) : 513-521.

Lee, J., 'A third division team?' Seirbhis Phoibli 6
    (1:1985) : 3-8.

Livingston, W., 'Britain and America: The
    institutionalization of accountability,' Journal of
    Politics (November 1976) : 879-894.

MacSharry, R., 'The White Paper "Serving the Country
    Better" -- A step in the right direction,' Seirbhis
    Phoibli 7 (1:1986): 3-6.

McKinnell, J., and L. Howard, Public Administration:
    Balancing Power and Accountability. Illinois:
    Moore Publishing Co., 1979.

McNamara, T., 'Ethics and the civil service: Is it an
    issue?' Seirbhís Phoiblí 7 (4:1986): 8-14.

Maher,M., 'Accountability in governmental units,'
    Journal of Contemporary Business 6 (1:1977) : 7-
    17.

Maheshwari, S., 'Accountability in public administration:
    Towards a conceptual framework,' Indian Journal of
    Public Administration Vol. XXIX (3: 1983): 457-
    472.

Mosher, F., et al., Watergate: Implications for Responsible
    Government. New York: Basic Books, 1974.

Murphy, K., 'Raising productivity in the civil service,'
    Seirbhís Phoiblí 3 (1:1982) : 2-14.

Murray, C.H., 'A working and changeable instrument,'
    Administration 30 (4:1982): 43-73.

Nixon, J., 'Evaluating select committees and proposals
    for an alternative perspective,' Policy and
    Politics 14 (4:1986): 415-438.

Normanton, E., The Accountability and Audit of
    Governments. Manchester: Manchester University
    Press, 1966.

Normanton, E., 'Reform in the field of public
    accountability and audit: A progress report,'
    Political Quarterly 51 (April-June 1980) : 175-
    199.

O'Callaghan, D., 'Controlling the state-sponsored
    bodies,' Administration 31 (4:1983) : 346-371.

Office of the Ombudsman, First Report. Dublin:
    Stationery Office, 1985.

Office of the Ombudsman, Annual Report of the Ombudsman
    Ireland 1985. Dublin: Stationery Office, 1986.

O'Halpin, E., 'The Dail Committee of Public Accounts,
    1961-1980,' Administration 32 (4:1984) : 483-
    511.

Plehwe, R., 'Public administration by private agencies:
    A review article,' Australian Journal of Public
    Administration 35 (September 1976) : 251-257.

Price,C., 'Making a select committee work,' Public
    Money (March 1985) : 29-32.

Public Service Advisory Council, Report for the Year
    Ended 31 October 1980. Dublin: Stationery
    Office, 1981.

Public Service Advisory Council, Report for the Year
    Ended 31 October 1982. Dublin: Stationery
    Office, 1983.

Public Service Advisory Council, Report for the Year
    Ended 31 October 1983. Dublin: Stationery Office,
    1984.

Public Service Advisory Council, Report for the Year
    Ended 31 October 1984. Dublin: Stationery Office,
    1985.

Rawson, B., 'The responsibilities of the public servant
    to the public: Accessibility, fairness and
    efficiency,' Canadian Public Administration 27
    (4:1984) : 601-610.

Reddin, W., and Kehoe, P., Effective MBO for Irish
    Managers. Dublin: Mount Salus Press, 1974.

Report of the Public Services Organisation Review Group,
    1966-1969. Dublin: Stationery Office, 1969.

Ridley, F., 'The British civil service and politics:
    Principles in question and traditions in flux,'
    Parliamentary Affairs (36:1983) : 28-48.

Ridley, F., 'Who is the civil servant's master?,'
    New Society (14 June 1985).

Robinson, A., et al., 'Symposium on ministerial
    responsibility,' Public Administration 65 (Spring
    1987): 61-91.

Roche, R., 'The high cost of complaining Irish style: A
    preliminary examination of the Irish pattern of
    complaint behaviour and its associated costs,'
    IBAR 4 (October 1982) : 98-108.

Rosen, B., Holding Government Bureaucracies Accountable.
    New York: Praeger, 1982.

Seidler, L., and L. Seidler, Social Accounting:
    Theory, Issues and Cases. California: Melville,
    1976.

Seirbhis Phoibli, A Special Issue on the White Paper on
    the Public Service, Serving the Country Better, 6
    (Nollaig 1985).

Serving the Country Better. A White Paper on the Civil
    Service. Dublin: Stationery Office, 1985.

Sinnott, R., 'Interpretations of the Irish party system,'
    European Journal of Political Research   12 (1984)
    : 217-241.

Sharp, K., 'Evaluating "Value for Money",'   Management in
    Government   (4 : 1983 : 250-260.

Skene, G., 'Auditing efficiency and management in the New
    Zealand public sector,' Australian Journal of
    Public Administration   44 (3:1985): 270-286.

Smith, B., and J. Carroll, (eds), Improving the
    Accountability and Performance of
    Government. Washington D.C.: Brookings Institute,
    1982.

Smith, B., and D. Hague, (eds),   The Dilemma of
    Accountability in Modern Government.   London:
    Macmillan, 1971.

Smyth, W., 'The responsibility of the civil servant in
    Ireland,'   Administration   23 (4: 1975) : 339-361.

Starkie, D., 'Reassessing the impact of Select
    Committees,'   Public Administration Bulletin   (41
    : 1983) : 2-13.

Tetlock, P., 'Accountability: The neglected social
    context of judgement and choice,'   Research in
    Organisational Behaviour   Vol 7. JAI Press, 1985.

Thomas, R., 'The politics of efficiency and effectiveness
    in the British Civil Service,'   International
    Review of Administrative Sciences   (69 : 1) 1983 :
    239-251.

Turem, E., and J. Turem, 'The crisis of accountability,'
    Social Work (January 1974) : 5-16.

Walker, S., 'The basic structure of accountability and
    accountable management in Government departments,'
    Management Services in Government   34 (1979) : 13-
    21.

Welton, J., 'Accountability in educational
    organisations,' Educational Administration   9
    (Autumn 1980) : 25-41.

Williams, D., Maladministration: Remedies for
    Injustice.   London: Oyez, 1976.

Wright, M., 'The responsibility of the civil servant in Great Britain,' Administration 23 (4 : 1975) : 362-395.

Yardley, D., 'Local Ombudsmen in England: Recent trends and developments,' Public Law (Winter 1983): 522-531.

Young, J., 'Accountability in government: Many things to many people,' Bureaucrat (Spring 1980) : 17-20.